FILLING *The* VACUUM

ALTERNATIVE INVESTMENTS FOR PENSION PLANS, ENDOWMENTS AND FOUNDATIONS

INVESTORS
PRESS

Published in the United States by Investors Press.

Library of Congress Cataloging-in-Publication Data
    Investors Press
    Filling the Vacuum: Alternative Investments for Pension Plans,
                Endowments and Foundations/Investors Press
        ISBN 1-885123-02-7
        I. Filling the Vacuum: Alternative Investments for Pension Plans,
        Endowments and Foundations
Printed in Mexico

10 9   8   7   6   5   4   3   2   1

Jacket art and design © 1994 by Wendell Minor
Book design by Silver Communications Inc.
Endowment & Foundation Edition

ACKNOWLEDGEMENT

Investors Press is pleased to present **Filling the Vacuum**, the third of four books in its 1994 Investment Management Series.

Each of these original books examines issues of compelling concern to pension and investment officers, trustees, benefits administrators, pensions consultants and money managers. Each book is written by distinguished professionals in the field whose essays reflect their own independent and informed opinions.

Edited and published by Investors Press, this unique educational Series is made possible through the underwriting of a small group of leading firms to whom appreciation goes from everyone who values the importance of education and the candid exchange of information. Because of their vision and commitment, this new Series becomes a tool for the sharing of experience and insight and initiates an essential bridge between members of the investment community that encourages dialogue, discussion and deeper understanding.

INVESTORS
PRESS

1994 INVESTMENT MANAGEMENT
BOOK SERIES

Underwritten by

ANGELO, GORDON & CO.

BARINGS

CHICAGO BOARD OF TRADE

CHANCELLOR CAPITAL MANAGEMENT

THE DREYFUS TRUST COMPANY

FIDELITY INVESTMENTS

INSTINET

MERRILL LYNCH

METLIFE

NCM CAPITAL

TABLE OF CONTENTS

INTRODUCTION

As pension funds struggle in the 1990s to develop innovative investment strategies that enable them to meet their long-term obligations, all share a common reality: the rules of the game have changed. The dramatic double-digit returns of the '80s generated through traditional domestic investments are fast becoming mythical memories best described by a nostalgic "remember when..." Today, meeting and exceeding target goals of real rates of return require a new look at "risk," a new definition of "alternative," and a willingness to tap the myriad of opportunities that beckons from a bulging world of not so "alternative" alternative investments.

Only recently, alternative investments seemed to be the exotic playground of the trailblazers of the pension fund world. Their esoteric thinking and courageous commitment to a particular vision of the future seemed to make them smarter and gutsier than the majority of fiduciaries who sat, satisfied, on the safe side of innovation, contentedly riding out the whopping returns of the last decade.

But rethinking an entrenched, conservative approach to risk-taking, and redefining when "risk" is riskier to avoid than embrace, are now the operative rules for responsible retirement funds. More and more, innovation is originating on the plan sponsor side as pension fund managers increasingly exercise their ability and expertise to plant and nourish spin-offs of less traditional specialties.

Even the most staunchly conservative investment committees are peeling back layers of historic aversion to alternative investments. Current returns and future expectations that outpace performance from traditional asset classes are making alternatives the "third leg of the stool" as they balance the risk/return equation of equity and fixed income. Clearly, risk must be assessed in terms of portfolios as a whole.

But the media loves drama and controversy, and the feverish reporting of many venture capital debacles and real estate disasters continues to leave some investors wary. The massive derivatives losses that battered Procter & Gamble, as an example, give skeptics, who think CATS, COUGARs and SWAPS are an alphabet of Wall

Street mumbo-jumbo, a convenient "I told you so!" Other investors oppose pension funds' participation in economically targeted investing because they feel the ETI focus on social and economic development weakens the prudent investor's mission to seek returns solely for the benefit of plan participants.[1]

Controversy, fueled by public exposure, can always frighten even committed investors: as this book goes to press one chapter written with great candor by the head of a large state retirement system could not be completed when his aggressive — and successful — alternative investment program became, unexpectedly, the target of a political candidate's attack.

Filling the Vacuum: *Alternative Investments for Pension Plans, Endowments and Foundations*, the third book in Investors Press' four-part 1994 Investment Management Series, delivers the compelling message that the expanding choices offered by alternative investments have, indeed, entered the "mainstream" of investment opportunities. No longer viable for only the largest retirement funds, the gamut of these investment alternatives has gained greater understanding, respectability — and use — among a wide range of pension funds, endowments and foundations. The drawbridge is down: everyone is welcome.

Our distinguished authors illustrate with simple and understandable examples how they navigate the roiling waters of alternative investing with skill, pragmatism and prudence. **Tom Judge**, AT&T's Vice President and Director of Alternative Investments, gives an overview of venture capital and shares his long-term perspective of this asset class. **Douglas Park**, Director, Private Transactions/Venture Capital, writes about Ameritech's commitment to private placements and LBOs while **David White**, Treasurer and Chief Investment Officer of The Rockefeller Foundation details his fund's involvement in hedge funds and **Erica Bushner**, Director of Venture Capital and Alternative Investments for the Pennsylvania State Employes' Retirement System analyzes her fund's involvement in ETIs. **Sallie Shuping Russell**, Vice President and Investment Director of the Duke Management Company, considers asset allocation strategies for alternative investments generally, **David VanBenschoten**, Vice President, Director of Finance – Investments at General Mills details a practical approach to derivatives, **Carmen Gigliotti**, Portfolio Manager, Venture Investments at DuPont, describes his fund's changing view of distressed debt opportunities and **Richard Rose**, Chief Investment Officer, reveals an insider's view of the San Diego County Employees' Retirement Association's managed futures program.

From these actual case studies readers learn the brief history of each author's involvement with alternative investing, the structure of their programs and how each uses his or her in-house staff and their consultants. And to give even the most skeptical investor a better understanding and higher comfort level about alternative investing, our authors pay great attention to describing their due diligence process, sharing insights and guidance about the steps they follow to ensure that they are, indeed, acting in the best interests of their plan participants.

Several of the authors are extraordinarily candid about their past mistakes and

---

[1] See "From Pacifist to Activist: The New Breed of Public Fund Trustee," by Peter D. Ashe, Chairman of the Board, San Francisco City and County Employees, **The Changing Face of Pension Management**, Investors Press, 1994, pp. 25-41.

the struggles they surmounted in winning investment committee approval for alternative investing. Many discuss mentors and advisors who guided their efforts, and *all warn readers about the pitfalls* to avoid. Our authors also offer a series of straightforward "smart pills" to welcome the uninitiated to their strong and supportive network of venture capital investors.

Filling the Vacuum does not include yesterday's news. For example, our authors write comparatively little about international or real estate investments, two very important components of the asset allocation model, even though many plans still have lingering needs for information on these and other investment areas that have become relatively commonplace. Instead, this important book focuses on today and tomorrow, and the alternative investments that are still being explored, tested and questioned by many plan sponsors.

The purpose of this book is not to translate complex derivatives formulas or debate the ethics of economically targeted investments, but to give readers the practical information they need to consider alternative investments as a viable asset class, choose partners or advisors wisely and devise thoughtful, innovative strategies that help you meet your long-term needs and goals.

We have invited plan sponsors nationwide to share with our readers their experience and knowledge of alternative investments which, as you develop innovative strategies for the future, may very well become primary, rather than alternative, asset classes in your plan's asset allocation mix.

In addition to the important insights and guidance shared by our authors, Investors Press includes an important Resource Guide designed to increase the book's ongoing usefulness and reference value. As part of this important and innovative educational project, **Filling the Vacuum** continues the standard of excellence, clarity and candor established by **The Changing Face of Pension Management** and **A Wing and a Prayer**, the first two books in the Series.

Kathryn A. Sollmann
Managing Editor
Investors Press
Washington, Connecticut

CHAPTER
ONE

AT&T's Mainstream Equity Investment in Venture Capital

Tom Judge

When AT&T made its first venture capital investment in 1980 the market bore little resemblance to today's relatively bustling private equity sector.

Pension plans and other institutional investors as a group really weren't in private equity in the 1970s. The venture capital business was a field in its adolescence: much of its money was relatively inconsequential and came from individuals. As a result, the sector itself was small and not geared toward the institutional marketplace.

Although AT&T broke from the classic stock-bond scenario in the early 1970s when we started investing in real estate, and continued afterward to look for other ways to enhance the return in our portfolio, it was not clear to us that venture capital and private equity, generally, were really areas where pension funds belonged.

But all that was about to change. In the late 1970s two things happened that opened the door for pension funds to jump into venture capital investing. *First*, the capital gains tax was lowered. That may not seem like a significant development to a tax-exempt plan, but it had profound effects on venture capital. In order to entice quality people to give up good jobs and join small start-up companies that might or might not make it, there had to be a tasty enough carrot to attract them. The carrot wasn't salary or perks: it was the opportunity down the road to make *a lot of money*. One of the things preventing that had been the high capital gains tax.

Second was the clarification by the DOL of the prudent man rule under ERISA. For the first time, pension plans were given a clear sign that venture capital and other alternative investments were appropriate assets for prudent pension managers. Together, these two pivotal changes attracted quite a few pension investors into venture capital partnerships.

For a neophyte, however, it wasn't easy to approach the market in those days. We didn't know too much about the business back then and, unfortunately, we weren't alone. There weren't too many people at both institutions and asset management firms who knew anything about venture capital in 1980, so there weren't many places to turn for advice. Of course, everything is different now.

Today, the industry even has a support group for institutional investors. Founded in 1990, the Institutional Limited Partners Association currently includes almost 45 institutions and meets twice a year to discuss important issues of interest to today's institutional alternative asset investor.

In 1980, there was no such group. There was not the proliferation of gatekeepers, consultants and other experts available today. I was fortunate, however, to establish a relationship early on with Ray Held who had made a number of venture capital investments at Manufacturers Hanover in the 1970s. In those first few years, he taught me a lot about venture capital and I taught him a lot about what makes institutional investors tick. And that relationship, which started with Manufacturers Hanover and moved to Mitchell Hutchins when the Manny Hanny asset management operations were acquired, was in place until several years ago when we brought our venture capital management in-house. Even then, that decision was purely economical: my management committee was convinced that I could do every bit as good a job with the portfolio for one-third the cost by bringing it in-house. So far, that's been true.

Along the way, we also changed the structure of our private equity investing program by separating buyouts and venture capital partnerships. It should be noted, however, that there is much common ground between the two and the split was purely arbitrary. Until the late 1980s, in fact, we had the two together under one program, but then we realized it just didn't make sense for the same people to track every single investment we had.

VENTURE CAPITAL: PART OF AT&T's EQUITY PORTFOLIO

It should also be pointed out that we don't view venture capital as an asset class. To AT&T, venture capital is part of our equity portfolio. There are a lot of ways you can look at your portfolio: as liquid vs. illiquid investments, passive vs. active, etc. We look at our portfolio as equity, fixed income and real assets. If you only have those three buckets, venture capital has to go in your equity portfolio.

It was within that context that we first approached venture capital in 1980. We saw it simply as a way of enhancing our equity returns. Venture capital at the time was a very small, very informal market. Not only did most institutional investors not really know much about venture capitalists, venture capitalists didn't really know much about us, either. The venture capitalists really didn't understand an institutional investor's mindset or needs. We weren't driven by interesting companies and deals: we were driven by returns.

We learned very early on, however, that the returns were not quite as phenomenal as they were hyped up to be. You realized pretty quickly that you only heard about the big winners. You never heard about the money lost, and we learned fast that a lot of money was lost. The returns thrown around in the 35% range were actually on individual deals; actual returns on average, while still good, were considerably lower than that.

For instance, our current return expectations for venture capital are 15%, just 500 basis points above our long-term return expectations for domestic common stock. In fact, over optimistic return expectations for venture capital are common in the institutional investor community. A good rule of thumb is to expect your venture capital returns to run about 300 to 500 basis points over domestic stocks.

It should be noted, as well, that performance measurement can present difficulties in and of itself. First, funds typically show little or no return in the early years of the partnership, often resulting in the "J-curve" phenomenon: low to negative returns in the early years as capital calls and early investments are made, followed by a quick ramp up in returns in later years as the early investments begin to pay off.

For that reason there's a lot of hue and cry in the venture capital community about how we should not measure returns early in a fund's life. But it's like keeping score in a baseball game — you keep score at the end of each inning. You don't wait until the end of the game to find out who's winning and losing.

CAPITAL OVERFLOW, KNOWLEDGE DEFICIT

Of course, we learned other lessons over the intervening 14 years and, in fact, many of them were learned just a few years after we kicked off our program. From 1983 to 1985 lots of money was thrown at the industry, money the market just couldn't handle. Essentially, people who were not really venture capitalists came out and raised venture capital funds and, unfortunately, we funded some of those. Compounding the problem of inexperienced managers was the overflow of capital in the market. Too much money chasing too few deals resulted in a classic supply-demand imbalance, bidding up private valuations and watering down overall returns.

Frankly, I am concerned today about the recent influx of so much new capital into the market. After a long dry period, the industry is starting to see a lot of new money, both from long-dormant players and from many new faces. In the 1980s, the stock market was yielding 17 to 18% per year on average. Now investors are expecting returns of 10% or slightly less, so a lot of them are looking for investments with a higher return. One of the things they're finding is venture capital.

It's really the new investors who worry me because they don't understand how to put their money to work in this market. Some of the very large state pension funds have decided to go into venture capital, but they've gone about it by putting x% of

Put your nose on Kansas.

Now you see the U.S. the way most domestic asset managers do.

A little too closely.

In today's global economy, domestic portfolios of all countries are heavily influenced by international markets and events. A purely domestic approach to managing these portfolios is as obsolete as the passbook savings account.

Whether you're investing domestically or internationally, what you need is a whole-world perspective.

With regional specialists in all major markets, Barings gives you a more complete and accurate view of investment opportunities anywhere.

A view you'll find nowhere else.

Today, there are no longer "domestic" or "international" managers.

There are simply those who can help you succeed in the world as it is now.

And those who can't.

For more on the unique advantages of Barings' global approach to investment management, call Fraser Blakely at 617-951-0052.

BARINGS

their assets to work over y number of years. They'll try to put a lot of money to work over a very short period of time. People think it's easy to set an allocation target and meet it. Well, I've got news for them — it's not easy. In fact, it may be impossible.

For example, since January 1980 AT&T has committed $1.3 billion to venture capital. About two-thirds of that, roughly $835 million, has been called. But about 70% of it has been distributed back. So, with a $1.3 billion commitment, we've got a portfolio worth $255 million on a cost basis and $680 million at market value. Even though we're trying to put more money to work in venture capital, because of the distributions it's very difficult to increase our percentage exposure.

CAUTION AND SELECTIVITY

What all this new money means to us is that we have to be more cautious. Although we do not, and have never, timed our way in and out of the market even when we feel it might be getting overheated, in this environment we cannot lose sight of maximum selectivity. We must satisfy ourselves that the general partners we invest in will be as selective as possible in choosing their deals.

Our activity is often driven by what's going on in the market, but we invest only in partnerships we want to be in regardless of when they come to market. It would be nice to tell people we dollar average but you can't dollar average in the venture capital market. We invest over time but what determines how much money we put in the market is which firms are raising money. We invest in the best firms in the business. If they're all raising money in a given year, we'd probably invest a lot more than average. If none of the quality firms is raising money in a given year, we probably would not commit a dime.

DUE DILIGENCE: CHOOSING THE OPPORTUNITY

How do we decide whom to wait for and whom to reject? As a result of earlier market difficulties, we are *highly selective*. We have developed a sophisticated system of due diligence and today we are far more careful about whom we will fund. *Now we look for experienced venture capitalists.* We look for individual general partners who have been through good and bad times, who've made mistakes and learned from those mistakes. We look for venture capital experience and we look for operating experience. We are finding more and more in the venture capital field that operating experience is crucial, as contrasted to the buyouts arena where financial expertise may be more important.

One thing that is unique about venture capital investing is that the track record of an individual general partner is a good indicator of future performance. That is not necessarily true of any other investment area but it is true here because these professionals have tested experience. They've been through the entire process and they've learned what not to do.

We also look for team experience; we want to be sure these people can work together as a group. People in this business have big egos. Although there's nothing wrong with that and it might even help, we need to make sure it's not going to get in the way of the fund's performance. We don't want to invest in a partnership that's going to blow apart. We always make sure they have a well developed decision-making process that results in well-structured deals.

Deal flow is also an important element of sound decision-making. The key question is: where is their deal flow coming from? Once again, experience is important. People who have been in the business a long time have established networks; they're not getting the ordinary deals everybody else sees.

Another issue is the general partner's previous fund. Did they actually do what they said they were going to do? Does the fund reflect their strategy? We address the issue of performance here. Although the venture capitalists don't like to talk about performance, we think it's essential and important.

Performance also raises the issue of benchmarking or looking, not just at absolute returns, but at how those returns stack up relative to similar funds. We believe in vintage year performance measurement and comparison. All the funds raised at the same time were operating in the same economic environment, so I think it's a valid relative measurement. A lot of people benchmark against the general Venture Economics Index but I don't think that makes sense. The Venture Economics Index measures the universe of venture capital and you don't want to invest in the whole universe.

We also scrutinize the product, or the fund strategy. Is the product or strategy well-designed? Does it make sense? Is the firm innovative? Is it a haven for new ideas? All of these are important considerations.

Finally, we look at price. If the partnership is small and focused on labor-intensive early stage and seed investments, management fees as high as 3% per year might be appropriate. But for most funds, the fees should be much lower. I think up to 1.5% in the early part of the fund when not much money has been put to work, 2.5% when the partnership is most active, and trailing off thereafter are probably correct levels. I am a strong believer that management fees should only cover reasonable costs; they should not be a profit center.

Often you don't have much leverage in negotiating price. It doesn't always depend on the popularity of a given fund, as you might think, but rather on the philosophy of the general partners. In the past year, one group came out to raise a fund and announced ahead of time that they would not discuss terms or conditions. I don't think that's appropriate, but it is a real reflection that what it can come down to is how much respect the general partners have for their limited partners. Over the years I've realized that the human element of venture capital investing — trust and respect — often bring the greatest long-term results.

➤ Don't set your return expectations too high. AT&T's current return expectation on domestic common stock is 10% and on venture capital 15%. Don't expect more than 300 to 500 basis points over domestic public equities.

➤ Don't expect to put a lot of money in venture capital over a short period of time.

➤ Don't treat venture capital as an asset class. If you have to go to your investment committee to sell the concept as an asset class, it's a difficult task. I suggest selling it as equity.

➤ Keep in mind that venture capital, unlike most other investments, throws off distributions.

➤ It is the long-term record of your portfolio that counts, not short-term results.

➤ Choose venture capital firms you would entrust with your own money.

Imagine this: You're reallocating equity assets: selling Japan,

Malaysia and Hong Kong; buying the U.K., Holland and Finland. You need it done

[direct, local access in over 30 countries]

today–100% completion. What's more, three of the orders represent more than two

[the difficult trades]

days' average volume. You need to protect your profile, and you need local liquidity

[anonymity reduces market impact]

and best execution in all six markets–now. How are you going to do this? There's only

[a complete transaction analysis service]

one choice: access order flow directly and reach local brokers and exchanges, global

[the neutrality of a global agency broker]

institutions and wholesalers all at the same time. To complete the trades, balance

[instant, simultaneous communication]

the cash, receive more trading information and fulfill some research commitments–

[a worldwide soft commission capability]

You're going to Instinet.

[for information call 800-225-5008]

This is trading.

Instinet clients. Focused on performance.

The Asset Allocation Pie: Duke's Long-Term Big Slice of Alternative Investments

Sallie Shuping Russell

Duke Management Company differs from most other plan sponsors because we don't consider alternative assets to be alternative. In fact, to us, they're very much mainstream.

In contrast to most institutional investors, who commit approximately 5% to "alternative assets," we have almost one-third of our portfolio allocated to them. That number surprises a lot of people but if you look at the history of our plan and the way we built our asset allocation model it makes a lot of sense.

Our program is deeply rooted in our status as a university fund manager: to understand the rationale behind our asset allocation model, you must understand the particular characteristics and needs of endowments.

INVESTING FOR PERPETUITY

A university endowment is the quintessential long-term investor since it has to support the institution in perpetuity. As a result, subject to cash requirements, it is best for endowments to look at their portfolios and their investment decisions on a total return basis rather than on an income-only basis. In other words, *the main concern for the Duke University endowment is to protect its purchasing power, to meet the spending needs of the university while offsetting the erosion of inflation.*

At the same time, however, an endowment does have need for some liquidity. The typical university requires 4 to 6% of its endowment every year to meet its spending needs. With the goal of keeping the purchasing power of its principal intact, that spending figure equals an endowment's real return hurdle. It was with all of that in mind that our asset allocation model was built in early 1985.

Actually, by 1985 Duke had already been investing in alternative assets for seven years. The university made its first investments in private equity in 1978 thanks largely to the efforts of the university's president, Terry Sanford and several innovative trustees. President Sanford and members of the Trustee Investment Committee were true believers in alternative assets and, even though the program was pursued on a case-by-case basis until the mid-1980s, Duke had a relatively high allocation of 5 to 10% to these assets during that period.

When we started looking at the numbers in 1985, however, it soon became clear that a 5 to 10% commitment wouldn't be enough. The university had targeted its spending needs at 5.5% of the endowment per annum. We were faced, therefore, with a dilemma: historically, equities had long-term returns after inflation of only 5 to 5.5%; fixed income promised even less — a paltry 3% real return. We could probably get to our real return target by placing the entire portfolio in equities, but obviously that would be neither prudent nor feasible.

A Major Commitment to Alternative Investments

In order to obtain an equity level of returns — but with lower overall risk — we started looking for assets with high expected real returns and low correlations with equity returns. Alternative assets seemed a perfect choice: we projected they would hit a 6 to 10% real return and their low correlation with traditional asset classes made them a great diversification play. Accordingly, we set the allocation for venture capital at 10% of assets, leveraged buyouts at 5%, real estate at 10%, and oil and gas at 5%.

Since that time, we have added a 15% allocation for what we term "opportunistic" investments. The opportunistic category is exactly what it sounds like — investments with a high return possibility that are essentially point-in-time phenomena. Because many hedge funds invest with that same philosophy, we place them within the opportunistic category and, in fact, they comprise one-half of our 15% allocation. Other funds in that category include our distressed securities partnerships which capitalize on the stream of bankruptcies and restructurings that has flowed over the past several years.

In 1990 we merged the LBO and venture capital asset classes to reflect a convergence in the two markets. Many LBO investors, in the face of tightened credit markets, had abandoned their financial architecture strategies in favor of hands-on, value-added investing. Many venture capitalists, burned by the high-risk, high-return classic venture model, had shifted away from using traditional start-up capital to more risk-averse, later-stage and buyout methodologies. Merging these strategies allowed us to focus less on financing techniques and more on industry stage or lifecycle opportunities.

Recently, however, we reduced our private equity allocation from 15% to 12.5%. Ironically, though we still favor this asset class, we just couldn't put that money to work productively on a rapid time horizon. Right now, we have 10% invested in 56 partnerships, a fairly large portfolio to manage. Moving forward, we expect to invest more money in fewer partnerships and believe we can reach our 12.5% target comfortably by the end of 1995.

Even with that recent reduction, many may see our allocation as a startlingly high commitment to the asset class and wonder how we got our trustees to support it. There's a story behind that, too.

Building Support for Alternative Investments:
The Duke Management Company

First, let me say that Duke has great trustees. We have been blessed with several who are savvy investors and others who are savvy enough to know they are not. But even if we didn't have the trustees we have, I think our experience in the 1987 stock market crash would have convinced any trustee group to give us a little more room to maneuver.

In that long summer of 1987 we, like many institutions at the time, put in place a portfolio insurance plan. Essentially, we hedged about one-fifth of the portfolio, about $100 million at the time, with financial futures. Late in the summer, as options prices came off, we switched to an options-based strategy, which was cheaper and gave us a pure hedge.

When the market fell out of bed in October, we were suddenly sitting on options that had cost us about $1 million and were now worth about 15 times that. We decided immediately that we should liquidate the position. Unfortunately, we didn't have the authority to sell without the approval of the Investment Committee. While we were lining up authorization to sell the options, their prices slipped substantially to about nine times cost. We still made money on the trade but it was a lesson that drove home the need for more rapid decision-making. This necessitated a more nimble internal management structure.

That experience led the trustees to reconsider the best organizational structure to exploit inefficiencies in today's capital markets. They agreed to invest in the creation of a professional management staff authorized to make investment decisions within a reasonable time limit. They also streamlined the approval process for investments outside these levels of authority. The result was the Duke Management Company, founded in 1989. Today we have a team of six investment professionals managing approximately $1.5 billion on a full-time basis.

So far, we don't think we've let the trustees or the university down. Since its inception, our private equity returns have exceeded 15% annualized, and this includes a number of partnerships still carried at cost. It is important to note, however, that during the "building phase" of a private equity portfolio, its returns will generally lag behind those of its public security counterparts. During this phase the private equity portfolio is inordinately weighted toward younger partnerships which have yet to register returns on their underlying investment portfolios. At Duke, we estimate this "drag effect" to have reduced our return on the overall endowment by up to 400 basis points for several years.

Now, however, as the partnership portfolio matures and becomes more balanced, it promises higher returns. In fact, for the past year the private equity portfolio has out-performed both the public equity portfolio and the endowment as a whole, logging a robust return of 25% for this fiscal year. This has reversed the earlier under-performance so that on a cumulative basis private equity has been very attractive relative to stocks and bonds. But *maintaining* a balance between mature investments, which are throwing off cash, and young funds, which are carried at cost or less (due to fees), is the challenge for successful private investing.

A BULLISH OUTLOOK

Moving forward, our outlook continues to be bullish. With today's easing of the credit markets, the buyout and mezzanine areas of the market should see greater opportunities. Increased competition for financing companies should result in more deals and fewer bankruptcies. The flip side, however, is that you will see fewer home runs.

Will the low yields on fixed income vehicles drive investors into the alternative asset class, glutting the market and driving up valuations while driving down yields? We *do worry* about the risk of that phenomenon because it has happened before. But we don't see danger signs on the near horizon. Instead, a low interest

Consider this:

As you study opportunities, you glide with ease

[for analysts, portfolio managers and traders]

between fundamental research, technical analysis, quotes, news, even real-time

trading–all on one screen. In fact, you've simplified the process even more

[the only fully integrated research and analytics service]

by organizing the information flow to fit your strategy. Click and up pops a list

[fully customizable indicators, signals and screens]

of stocks. A few clicks more and you've filtered the list through sets of fundamental

[access up to 10,000 issues]

and technical parameters that you've defined, quickly paring it to a few select

[screen, sort and rank lists using any combination of data]

candidates. Then you drag and drop these remaining symbols into the charting

window; instantly, you see buy/sell signals and price and volume trends ranging

[customize charts using available indicators or your own]

from intra-day to 13 years. A call for additional expertise is always available. You

[work with a pro-active research and analytics desk]

snap into the trading window, determine activity in each stock and set your

[trade through Instinet in real-time]

strategies. You're closing the gap between information and execution.

You're working with Instinet.

[for information call 800-225-5008]

This is research

INSTINET
A REUTER COMPANY

Instinet clients. Focused on performance.

rate environment is more likely to impact large-cap stocks and real estate since most investors concerned with current interest rates are also concerned with generating current income — and private equity is not a place for someone with liquidity needs.

While we're very happy with the results of our alternative asset investing program, don't make the mistake of thinking this success has come easily. *Alternative investing is a very labor-intensive process and we have put considerable effort into building our portfolio.*

DUE DILIGENCE: A CRITICAL INGREDIENT FOR SUCCESS

Due diligence regarding the partnership and its management is a crucial step in the investment process. While we use consultants for some due diligence and individual situations support, most of the work is completed in-house by the investment professionals on staff.

The first thing we look at in our due diligence process is the strategy of a proposed fund and whether it fits into what we want to do in Duke's portfolio. We firmly believe that in order to build a successful portfolio you have to plan ahead. You should know what you're going to do over the next 12-18 months. While there is room to be opportunistic in your fund investment strategy, well-planned portfolio decisions ensure that you are exposed to the areas of the market in which you want to participate, and have that exposure in place when the market makes its upward move.

For instance, we think that the large leveraged buyout fund market is liable to get overheated before we can get additional money to work, so we're not looking for any funds in that category other than those we have already identified. We are not looking at new middle-market buyout funds either because that's an area where we have enough current exposure. We will look at all proposals that come in the door but we won't invest in an area where we already have enough exposure or we think the opportunity is overplayed. I have a rule of thumb about the timeliness of fund strategies: if three to five prospectuses cross my desk with the same idea, the opportunity has probably passed and so should we!

Right now, our partnership portfolio planning model maps out five major and three opportunistic categories. The primary categories are seed and early stage investments, expansion capital including mezzanine debt, mature companies, restructurings and diverse partnerships. In addition to these broad categories, we have strategically targeted healthcare, communications and insurance as areas of interest for specific, opportunistic fund strategies. We invest in international funds as part of these subsets. Currently we have exposure in Western Europe and Asia, and continue to look at deals in Eastern Europe and Latin America.

Looking beyond the strategy of the fund, our next step in the due diligence process is to study the management team. We look at the people and their experience, not as individuals, but as a team. We need to be sure the partners can work together. We also look at their reputation, both in the operations and in the "deal" community. We want to know that people we respect would call the partners in this fund to participate in a deal. We also need to ensure that these are people entrepreneurs would call for backing.

Then we look at return. Obviously, great returns on a string of previous funds is a plus. But we also want to stress that poor returns in a prior fund are not necessarily a deal buster. There's a certain amount of gut feeling involved but the hard factors we look at include: what went wrong in the first fund? What did they do to correct it? What do people in the community think of them? Do they realize what went wrong and acknowledge their mistakes? How have they changed their organization or methodology to correct these mistakes? Often, failure is a good motivator. You can learn a lot from it.

Actually, there are very few absolute deal busters for us and they usually have to do with conflict and fee issues. In terms of conflicts, we are obviously uncomfortable with a general partner whose firm is also doing investment banking work for port-folio companies. In such cases, one can imagine (or experience!) a case where the general partner keeps a bad company afloat to generate additional banking fees. This is clearly a conflict with his activities as a principal investor. As for fees, we usually have no problem with the standard 2.5% management fee and 20% carried interest pricing structure, although we would obviously prefer to see lower pricing. What really kills a deal for us is paying placement fees, especially when an unsolicited proposal comes in. In our opinion, there's no reason why we should pay someone to sell a fund to us.

So far, however, placement fees haven't been much of an issue; most partner-ships interested in selling to us have been willing to waive the fee when we've said we won't pay it. In fact, partnership terms are generally the last thing we look at because we know they are always negotiable.

Beyond portfolio planning and thorough due diligence, the most important thing for an institution interested in alternative assets is to remember: if you're going to be in this market, you have to be a player. The biggest challenge in the alternative asset class is to make sure you get in with the right people and get the right deals. One of the best ways to do that is to stay in the market. *You have to invest over time. You have to be a presence in the market.* It's like anything else — if people know you're a long-term investor, they'll ask you to play in their game.

S M A R T   P I L L S

- ➤ Plan ahead for the next 12 to 18 months to be sure you're buying exposure in all the market sectors you want to be in.

- ➤ Consider alternative investing as a long-term investment policy and a permanent part of your institutional portfolio.

- ➤ Make sure your partnership managers are people who would be on the A-list of other venture capitalists and entrepreneurs.

- ➤ If three to five prospectuses cross your desk with the same idea, the opportunity has probably passed and so should you.

- ➤ Be patient; you will not see a return on investment for at least two years, and probably not until year five.

- ➤ Be a player. Don't try to time this market by going in and out. It will kill you — with a slow and painful death!

A growing number of non-profit institutions are re-examining their approach to investment management. Disenchanted with conventional thinking–and low investment returns– they are moving to the investment performance of Fidelity funds.

The advantages are obvious. At a time when maximum investment performance is increasingly vital, Fidelity delivers the quality of investment management you need.

With our wide variety of funds–offered

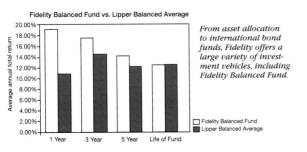

Fidelity Balanced Fund vs. Lipper Balanced Average

From asset allocation to international bond funds, Fidelity offers a large variety of investment vehicles, including Fidelity Balanced Fund.

no-load to non-profit institutions*–we can tailor creative and flexible solutions to your needs including cash and working capital, planned giving programs, endowment funds, defined benefit and deferred compensation plans.

Don't just hope for better returns. Pursue them actively.

What's more, given Fidelity's long experience in working with the non-profit community, you can expect well-informed and collaborative service. Service that will cut your

Fidelity's non-profit expertise ensures you a high degree of efficient, interactive service. We can help you reduce costs and boost productivity.

costs of administration and improve productivity.

We urge you to compare Fidelity with whomever you're using now. We will be happy to review your current investment performance, asset allocation and service costs.

If the time has come to pursue success more actively, it's time for Fidelity. Call Thom Bieniek, Senior Vice President, Fidelity Tax-Exempt Services Company, 1-800-841-3363.

Fidelity Investments®

THE ACTIVE PURSUIT OF SUCCESS

A Conservative Investor's Guide:
Customized Returns from Off-the-Rack Derivatives

David B. VanBenschoten

In 1994, "derivatives" replaced junk bonds and leveraged buyouts as the bogeymen of financial markets. Congress has held hearings; the SEC is pushing for regulation. Companies such as Procter & Gamble, Air Products and Chemicals, Dell Computer, Gibson Greetings, and Mead reportedly lost hundreds of millions of dollars on derivatives at stockholders' expense, while pension fund losses were posted by ARCO and the state of Louisiana, among others.

But despite all the bad press, with a total market size estimated at $12 trillion, derivatives aren't going away: they're simply too valuable a tool. In a 1994 *Fortune* magazine survey, 92% of the CEOs of 200 major U.S. companies said they would continue to use derivatives; there is no reason to doubt that they will.

CEOs recognize that derivatives are powerful tools that can accomplish tremendous results if used properly. They're like hammers and saws; they can build a beautiful house or cause tremendous damage. We've used derivatives for years, avoiding disasters while substantially boosting our overall returns.

To use derivatives wisely, you must understand how they work. More fundamentally, you must know what they are: financial arrangements whose values are linked to, or derived from, underlying assets such as stocks, bonds, commodities and currencies.

Consider, for example, that a baker wants to lock in the cost of flour for six months, reducing the risk that a shortage will drive up prices. Across town, a miller also wants to lock in flour prices, reducing the risk that a surplus will drive them down. They enter into a contract to buy and sell flour at a given price. That contract is a derivative.

Taking derivatives one step further, such forward agreements were standardized and offered by third parties, such as commodities exchanges, to facilitate trading. Originally, most futures contracts were for the delivery of grains and precious metals; they've been around for hundreds of years and are quite well developed in the U.S.

There's 1 in every crowd.

The world is full of also-rans. But in every category there's always a leader. Just one.

In retirement services, that title is held by Fidelity. But we didn't give ourselves that title. You did. The fact is, more companies trust Fidelity for their defined contribution plan needs than any other — half the Fortune 500 alone.

It isn't hard to see why. Fidelity takes the extra measures that keep you out in front. Not only in investment practices, but in technology, service, and innovation. Take a long look at your own plan needs. Ask yourself if your participants deserve the services of a leader, or of a follower.

Then call Peter J. Smail, Senior Vice President, Sales (617) 330-0335.

Fidelity Institutional Retirement Services Company
82 Devonshire Street, ZZ6, Boston, MA 02109

MAINSTREAM DERIVATIVES:
EXCHANGE-TRADED FUTURES AND OPTIONS

At General Mills, we have been using such derivatives for decades, an obvious outgrowth of our operations in agricultural markets. We were then well-prepared for the introduction of financial futures covering commodities like foreign currencies and Treasury bonds that have appeared in recent years.

In the early 1980s, U.S. stock index futures became available. Instead of buying the stocks of companies comprising the S&P 500, you could buy a contract representing those stocks. Since then, stock index futures on other major indexes, as well as on specific market sectors, have begun to trade.

Within a few months of their introduction, we began using stock index futures, the first derivatives in our pension fund. Because of our background in grain trading we are able to judge how these contracts are priced. We understand that the fair price of a futures contract has to have a direct relationship to the underlying asset's price. Incorporating factors such as carrying costs, dividends and interest rates, we calculate a theoretical fair value of the futures contract and compare it to the actual market price.

Sometimes stock index futures are priced high relative to the value of the underlying stocks, and sometimes they're priced low. When they're low-priced, we buy. If it's cheaper to hold our U.S. stock exposure in futures, rather than owning all the stocks in the S&P 500, we buy the futures. In effect, we can buy the S&P 500 or another stock index at a bargain price. *Of course, we only buy futures contracts on stocks that we'd want to own anyway as part of our basic portfolio strategy.*

Since the introduction of stock index futures, we've broadened our involvement in derivatives to include other instruments, primarily exchange-traded futures, but also options. Options permit you to skew your risks and your potential reward. Depending on whether you're buying or selling a put (option to sell) or a call (option to buy), you're either paying or receiving a fixed price. If you pay a

fixed price, you cut off your downside and fully participate on the upside. If you receive the fixed price, you're cutting off your upside with full exposure to losses.

Today, options are available on futures contracts as well as on the underlying commodities. Just as is the case with futures, some options are overpriced while others are underpriced. (Options tend to be priced on volatility. The greater the volatility, the greater the value, so options where true volatility is less than perceived volatility may be overpriced.)

STRUCTURING YOUR DERIVATIVES STRATEGY

Once you have the basic tools, you can build simple or complex structures. Suppose you want to buy stocks and options that are richly priced. In this case, you might sell puts. If stocks go up, as you anticipated, the puts will expire worthless and you're ahead only by the fixed amount of the premiums. If stocks go down, you have a loss (as you would have had by investing in stocks) but you're better off because you've received the put premiums.

If options are low-priced, you can buy calls. Say you hold 45% of your portfolio in stocks and you want to increase your allocation to 50%. Instead of investing 5% of your holdings directly into stocks, you can invest 5% in calls. You may have the same upside potential as if you were 70%-75% invested in stocks, but not as much downside.

After years of dealing with exchange-traded futures and options, we have determined that such derivatives are particularly valuable in asset allocation. Suppose, for example, that your portfolio allocation calls for 60% in stocks and 40% in bonds. You decide to move to a 50-50 mix. Normally that means selling stocks and buying bonds. Such trading generates transaction costs, generally 20 to 50 basis points for the buy and sell trades, even in the most efficient and liquid capital markets. This is a sizable amount for plan sponsors and, because of these costs, you would wait to make such moves until you felt extremely confident about your decision.

NCM Capital ...

On Equity Investing

"As a value manager, we believe that the security selection process begins with the identification of securities with low relative price earnings ratios."

I n the seven years since its founding, NCM Capital Management Group, Inc. has attracted a client base of some 70 employee benefit, foundation and endowment plans. With nearly $3 billion under management NCM Capital is one of the nation's most successful and well-respected minority owned investment advisory firms.

The firm offers a breadth of investment options which include equity, fixed income and balanced portfolio management. In all of its disciplines, the

On Fixed Income

"We believe that weighting corporates, particularly in the industrial and finance sectors, will add value to our portfolios."

Maceo K. Sloan,
Chairman, President and CEO

firm seeks to exceed respective index returns over a market cycle while maintaining a low risk profile. Additionally, it is the firm's goal to set the industry standard for client service.

To receive a detailed description of NCM Capital's investment

processes or additional information on how the firm can help you meet your own investment objectives, please phone or write:

Marc V. Reid
Tel (919) 688-0620
Fax (919) 683-1352

NCM Capital
Management Group, Inc.
103 West Main Street
Durham, NC 27701-3638

With exchange-traded derivatives, the cost of reallocating your portfolio drops to two to five basis points. The lower transaction cost either raises your return directly or permits you to reallocate assets more frequently, even if you're not as certain about the timing. Assuming you're right in your reallocation decision, you'll raise your return by such increased portfolio rebalancing.

In addition, we have found that using derivatives for asset allocation transactions can provide a "transportable alpha." Suppose you hire inside or outside investment managers. You've hired someone to pick stocks but then you make an asset allocation decision to cut back on stocks. That decision can interfere with the investment policies of the portfolio manager who wants, primarily, to buy the best stocks.

Using derivatives, you never create such conflicts with portfolio managers. You might sell stock index futures to effectively lighten up your stock allocation. Not only is this much cheaper than actually selling stocks and buying bonds, it allows your stock picker to keep on picking the best stocks. If he or she is right, you get to keep the value of those judgments even as you reduce the risk of the underlying asset class. Say the entire stock market is down by 10% while your selected stocks are down 5%. You earn the full 5% increment since the stock index futures you've sold will offset the broad market declines.

We implement this strategy using an overlay approach. That is, our in-house staff monitors the relationships between stocks and bonds, U.S. and international. We buy the asset class that has gone down and sell the asset class that has gone up, using exchange-traded derivatives. In the meantime, the portfolio managers we hire devote their full efforts to selecting the best assets.

THE QUEST FOR "TRANSPORTABLE ALPHA"

From there, we get to the concept I mentioned earlier, creating a "transportable alpha." Alpha is the extra value an active asset manager can add. Suppose I want to invest in stocks but I've hired the world's best bond manager. I'm convinced this manager can beat the bond market by 200 basis points each year but I need stock market exposure.

In this case, I'll have this manager continue to buy the physical bonds. Then I can sell bond futures and buy stock futures. In effect, I will have created a synthetic stock manager who's really a bond manager owning bonds, with a high alpha. By owning stock index futures, I will participate in any broad stock market appreciation. By selling bond futures while owning physical bonds, my return will be the alpha my bond picker provides. So I have stock market participation plus alpha —I've transferred the bond picker's alpha to the stock market.

Taking this concept to the ultimate degree, you can find anybody who can add value in any area. Then, using exchange-traded futures or other derivatives, you can create "transportable alpha." Just buy the underlying asset class you want to own and use any kind of manager and get the value-added from another class. You must also see the underlying asset class owned by the manager. This approach opens up the world to the best managers of any kind. You can use derivatives to get the exposure you want, along with the investment managers' capabilities in their underlying areas.

EXOTICA: OVER-THE-COUNTER DERIVATIVES

So far, I've discussed what might be called mainstream derivatives: exchange-traded futures and options. For such derivatives to be workable, you need standard contracts and generic underlying assets such as soybeans, corn, Treasury bonds, the S&P 500, etc. The more you get away from standardized underlying investments, the more the market thins out. Not everybody wants to invest in Italian stocks, for example. The same is true if you want a contract for a non-standard time frame.

In such cases, you're forced to go back to contractual arrangements between two parties, the original forward agreements illustrated by our baker-miller example. These are over-the-counter arrangements, with no exchange involved. They're customized contracts so the two parties can agree to any specifics they want. Exotic over-the-counter derivatives are the agreements that have received so much unfavorable publicity in 1994.

Suppose I wanted to buy stocks and sell bonds, and the underlying assets were noncustomized or illiquid. Instead of using two contracts, one to buy and one to sell, I could enter into a single agreement in which I could pay the return on whatever I'm selling and receive the return on what I'm buying. This is a swap agreement—two parties agree to trade returns on different investment vehicles.

The first over-the-counter derivatives were such swap agreements, often interest-rate swaps. These arrangements permit two parties to swap the returns on anything, or even several different things. Simple concepts can be used to build extremely complex structures.

At General Mills, we have not gone deeply into these complicated

PROCEED WITH CAUTION

The following types of exotic derivatives may not be perfect substitutes for traditional cash equivalents:

➤ Capped floaters: securities that don't pay any interest if market rates move above a certain level.

➤ CMT floaters: securities whose interest-rate reset provisions are tied to long-term interest rates, vulnerable to a change in the yield curve.

➤ COFI floaters: securities whose interest-rate reset provisions are tied to an index that materially lags behind short-term interest rates.

➤ Dual index floaters: securities whose interest-rate reset provisions are tied to a change in the relationship between two indexes.

➤ Inverse floaters and leveraged floaters: securities whose interest-rate reset provisions are based on a formula that magnifies changes in interest rates.

➤ Range floaters: securities that don't pay any interest if market rates move outside of a specified range.

derivatives. For one reason, exchange-traded derivatives are relatively inexpensive and you're dealing with a known party: the exchange. There are government regulations that provide known rules.

OFF-THE-RACK OR CUSTOM-MADE SUITS?

In the over-the-counter derivatives market there is a cost for customization. It's the difference between buying a $200 suit off the rack or a $1,400 custom-made suit from a superb tailor. The people who put over-the-counter derivatives together want to make a profit.

In general, we have not been willing to pay the price for customization. Our off-the-rack suits get the job done. Much of our activity is focused in exchange-traded derivatives. There's a clear market, you can see bids and asking prices, you know who you're dealing with and you have a regulatory structure in place.

Sometimes, though, someone else wants a custom made suit and the dealer who put together the arrangement wants to lay off some risk. In such cases, we have participated in over-the-counter derivatives. If we're willing to facilitate the trade, we can earn a profit by taking the other side.

EXTRA RISK

Over-the-counter derivatives have extra risks of which plan sponsors should be aware. The more complicated the derivative, the more difficult it is to tell what the ultimate price will be. So you should either deal with simple structures or use complicated derivatives you clearly understand. Most of the problems we've seen have resulted from people not understanding the complexity of the agreements they have entered into.

Often, with derivatives, you may not have to put up a great deal of cash. This might tempt you into larger agreements than would otherwise be the case. Avoiding or being cognizant of the high leverage that might be involved is another element of risk control.

If you're using derivatives to hedge a position you already have, or to take a position you normally would have taken, there's no incremental risk. Derivatives can even provide risk reduction. But others could take that same position and be speculating, not hedging. In 1994, some people were speculating on projected movements in interest rates; when they were wrong on the direction of interest rates, they lost money. With highly leveraged positions, they lost a lot of money when they were only slightly wrong.

GENERAL MILLS: DERIVATIVES AND THE FUTURE

At General Mills, we feel that the rewards of using derivatives have been worth the risks. For the past 10 years, while we have been moving between stock index futures and the underlying stocks, our maneuvering has probably added an 0.5% to 1% incremental return to our portfolio because we were in the cheaper vehicle.

Similarly, it has been much less expensive to implement our asset allocation strategies, saving 20 to 40 basis points a year in turnover costs. Our strategy has allowed us to make more frequent trades, probably adding another 20 to 40 basis points to our annual returns.

Based on our experience, we will continue to use derivatives. In the future, we may move more aggressively into over-the-counter derivatives. Although pension funds have gotten comfortable with swaps only in the last year or so, I am confident that most managers of pension funds, endowments, and foundations will be likely to use them to a significant degree. In addition, as international investing gains popularity, so will the use of derivatives outside the U.S. And I think you'll see the concept of "transportable alpha" become more widely understood and used.

To use derivatives wisely, focus first on the underlying investment. Then decide what form to use: derivatives or the underlying asset. Most of all, you have to understand the structure of the derivatives you may use. To lower your risks and enhance the rewards of derivatives, you should follow the guidelines that follow in the list of **Smart Pills**.

If you follow those guidelines, *you'll find that derivatives really aren't alternative investments at all. They are simply tools that can help you do a better job of doing what you have wanted to do all along.* On the other hand, if you decide simply to avoid derivatives, you may be asking for trouble: criticism can be waiting for you for not using derivatives if a capacity to hedge exists and you don't use it.

Derivatives are flexible enough to be applied to every kind of investment, exotic or plain. In addition to U.S. stocks and bonds, you can use derivatives to improve your performance with international stocks, international bonds, real estate, venture capital, as examples. Just as with any other tool, though, they must be in capable hands and there must be oversight to see that they are used properly. In the right hands, derivatives can provide truly the best of both worlds: less risk and greater rewards.

 S M A R T   P I L L S

- ➤ Know the costs of derivatives. Measure the difference between using the physical asset or the derivative.

- ➤ Be specific when pricing derivatives. Pricing derivatives requires computer models that use variables like possible future interest rates.

- ➤ Create "portable alpha." Separate the asset class decision from the decision of finding the best asset picker to add incremental value.

- ➤ Know whom you're dealing with. To the extent you use over-the-counter derivatives, you have to be concerned about your exposure to the other party's creditworthiness. For long-term arrangements, insist upon a AAA credit rating.

- ➤ Set rules for over-the-counter derivatives a dealer brings to you. You must be able to run derivatives offered to you through your pricing model.

- ➤ Be cautious with leverage. If you're going to be involved in leveraged transactions, learn the downside as well as the upside.

Defined by our commitment

to a disciplined, proven investment

process

Investing with Chancellor means
investing in a process—a clearly
defined, repeatable, rigorous
approach to asset management.
Our process is characterized by a
disciplined interplay of fundamental
and quantitative resources, developed and refined by the same group

The positive results of Chancellor's process are realized by our clients year after year: superior returns, controlled risk, and stable lasting relationships that genuinely contribute toward the fulfillment of client objectives.

Distinguished by our

superior long-term

results

 Chancellor Capital Management

A Patient Investor: Ameritech's Long-Term Buyout and Venture Capital Partnerships

Douglas K. Park

Today's low interest rate environment has prompted many pension funds to consider potentially high-return alternative investments for the first time, including buyout and venture capital limited partnership funds. Ironically, this particular asset class isn't a remedy for the current rate environment: because of its long lag-time between initial investment and ultimate return, you won't see a return from today's investment in buyout funds until at least five years from now — and with most venture capital investments, the lag is even longer.

Nonetheless, the surge of interest in venture capital and buyout limited partnership funds isn't misplaced. I strongly believe that in any rate environment this asset class is very appropriate for pension funds.

CHARACTERISTICS

➤ These are long-term investments and, therefore, naturally suited to a pension fund's long-term liability.

➤ They diversify portfolios because their timing and cash flows are so different from those of traditional investments.

➤ Historically, this asset class has provided higher long-term returns than the public markets.

For readers who have only a cursory knowledge of this asset class, perhaps some brief definitions are in order. *A venture capital limited partnership fund is a pool raised by a general partner for investment in promising start-up businesses and/or growth ventures.* The partners get shares in these ventures. If all goes well, the acquired companies do successful IPOs or become strategic acquisitions for other corporations. *A buyout fund invests in companies looking for capital to make key strategic, operational, or management changes that will boost their growth substantially.* Some buyout fund acquisitions are made with a relatively small down payment and loans for which the target firm's assets serve as security, and which will be repaid out of its cash flow. But today's buyouts aren't the highly leveraged, break-up value deals of the 1980s. *Today, the buyout business is about making growth acquisitions.* You don't want a company so over-leveraged that interest payments leave insufficient capital for growth.

The potential long-term net return in this asset class ranges between 15 and 20%. What's the downside risk? I may be biased, but I think it's pretty low. There's a big opportunity cost to a pension fund, of course, if its portfolio doesn't yield the expected returns. *But loss of capital is rare.* I don't think any partnerships have lost money, although I must qualify this by adding that few partnerships have yet been liquidated. The typical partnership runs at least ten years, with two- to three-year extensions. Some have lasted 15 years.

In fact, I'd like to see vehicles that would make these investments available to participants in defined contribution plans. One possible solution is to have a general partner's investments listed and traded in a public market so that plan participants could buy liquid shares. Another method might be to offer participants a diversified portfolio of which 95% consisted of traditional liquid investments, and 5% was in limited partnership assets.

AMERITECH: A PIONEER IN THIS AREA

Ameritech has been investing in venture capital and buyout limited partnership funds since 1984. We also make some direct investments on a co-investment basis — that is, we invest on equal terms with a partnership. Our current exposure in this asset class is about $500 million, or 5% of total pension fund assets. To date, our portfolio's IRR[1] over ten years is close to 14%. Based on my experience, I think it's realistic for investors to expect a net return between 15 and 20% *over periods of a decade or longer.*

Although a pioneer in this area, Ameritech stepped out of the market from mid-1990 through 1993 to reassess its portfolio and investment strategy. We understood that the main problem with this asset class is that it requires a lot of resources. Buyout and venture capital fund management fees have come down recently, but these are still high-cost, time-intensive, people-intensive investments. Since these assets represent only 5% of our total pension fund portfolio, we asked ourselves, "Is it really worth the hassle?"

Ameritech's decision was "Yes," for the reasons I mentioned earlier. Although this asset class represents only a small percentage of our total pension assets, it can generate a return 1,000 basis points higher than other classes, a sizable contribution to overall returns.

But the reassessment did refine our approach to the market. My responsibilities when I joined the company included establishing guidelines for diversification and selecting partnerships and direct investments consistent with a pension fund's needs.

You can establish parameters in which to work, but you have to stay flexible and keep looking at opportunities on a case-by-case basis. It's very difficult to create an asset allocation model in this class. There isn't enough data or history to create an index. We have tried to create a portfolio that will give us a broad

---

[1] Internal rate of return

exposure to the market. Our venture capital investments include both early and late-stage situations. In corporate finance we've focused on middle-market buy-outs, mezzanine investments[2] and in restructuring situations. Given the overall market size of buyouts versus venture capital, my base-line portfolio is 60/40, respectively.

We now have general criteria that a partnership must meet to qualify for our preliminary consideration. This is important because a basic screening process lets you consider 200 or 300 partnerships a year; without it you're forced to review each prospect in detail. If a partnership passes our first screen, we do due diligence on each company it has invested in in the past. Ameritech currently has 96 partnership funds; going forward, we intend to increase our participation in fewer funds so we won't have to monitor so many.

INTERNAL STRUCTURE

We have a dedicated internal staff of three investment professionals and one administrator. Because we have so many partnerships, we have also hired an outside firm — only to monitor and administer a portion of our portfolio. We were able to do this at a cost significantly lower than what you'd pay traditional gate-keepers who act as advisers.

Once a portfolio reaches about $100 million, a dedicated in-house staff becomes cost-effective. You might pay 50 basis points, or $500,000, to have an outsider manage that $100 million. You can hire two people and give them an appropriate travel budget for less than that. And an internal staff that focuses only on your assets is better able to customize deals for your specific needs than are gatekeepers who work for many clients. I also strongly recommend creating a separate investment committee for this asset class to expedite the day-to-day decision-making process.

CO-INVESTING

We think that co-investment is an excellent way to average down the cost of investing in this asset class over the long-term which, in turn, helps raise overall returns. Having the chance to say "yea" or "nay" to particular deals is a real benefit, like having a constant call option.

Admittedly, co-investing involves a lot more work than participating in a blind pool as a limited partner. Another drawback is that the pension fund deploys much less capital at a given time. If you only do direct investments, you're investing only a fraction of the money you can put into a limited partnership and you're taking on more risk. You lose diversification; as a direct investor you're making a single bet, where a partnership typically has some 15 investments. Finally, if you are co-investor on a well-known deal that goes under, you'll be exposed to some negative publicity.

But we believe the advantages of co-investing more than outweigh these drawbacks. The potential return is very high because you avoid the expenses you would have as a limited partner: the general partner's carried interest (i.e., his share of the fund's profits) and management fees, which can reduce your return by ten per-

---

[2] Subordinated debt

Although the performance of limited partnership funds tends to follow a "J" curve, our fund has followed an admittedly peculiar path in years one, two and three...

centage points. Co-investing leverages the general partner's knowledge. By becoming a limited partner you've bought his expertise but, as a limited partner, it's a resource you don't fully use. As a co-investor, you do. Ameritech currently does only two or three direct co-investments a year, but we'd like to reach the point where they represent 40% of our investments annually.

We also intend gradually to increase our allocation to this asset class from five to perhaps 15% of pension fund assets over a very long period of time. Ten years from now, I expect we'll have close to 10% of total assets invested in this class. To implement that decision properly, perhaps we'll widen our universe to include international as well as domestic venture capital. We currently have eight partnerships invested in U.K. funds and one or two in Asia, and are considering an appropriate international strategy.

PITFALLS TO AVOID

The biggest single pitfall for investors new to this asset class is their tendency to measure non-traditional assets in traditional terms. This thinking can paint a very distorted picture. For example, if you put this asset class into a traditional asset allocation model with its return expectations, standard deviations, etc., it will come out to a huge percentage of a pension fund. On a risk/return basis, correlated to other asset classes, this asset class looks like the best return for your money. You must constrain it artificially. A good analogy is the way real estate was considered, incorrectly, the perfect investment in the mid-1980s because it seemed to have high returns and low risk.

In the short-term, limited partnership funds can be highly volatile, so you have to be careful when you talk about returns on a time-weighted annual basis. The only accurate measurement is the IRR over a long period. When you assess a partnership's returns, for example, you should look at the net IRR to the limited partners and at the net

"Risk Arbitrage, Bankruptcy and Distressed Real Estate can be your least volatile investments in a prudently managed portfolio."

John M. Angelo, CEO
Angelo, Gordon & Co.

Risk Arbitrage, Bankruptcy

Angelo, Gordon defines risk arbitrage as "…situations with a begining, a middle and an analyzable conclusion." These are mostly short term investments in announced tenders and mergers.

Bankruptcy investment is considered in the same light but the conclusion can take from one to three years. Combining Risk Arbitrage and Bankruptcy results in portfolios of staggered maturities offering a predictable income stream.

Distressed Real Estate

Angelo, Gordon also specializes in distressed real estate assets, purchasing sub-performing and non-performing mortgages and properties. By prudent management of the underlying assets we are able to generate current yields of over 10% and expect all-in returns of over 20%. We focus on $5 to $20 million transactions—too big for most local real estate investors and too small for large capital pools.

Angelo, Gordon & Co.

Our portfolios are always diversified and typically unleveraged. Since our formation in 1988, we have continued to invest for our clients under a strict investment philosophy generating superior returns with low volatility.

If this thinking appeals to you, call John Angelo at **(212) 692-2020**.

Angelo, Gordon & Co. Experts in investments insulated from market fluctuation.

IRR to realized investments. If only one out of twenty investments has been liquidated, who knows what the ultimate value of the unliquidated investments will be?

It's also vital to remember that this asset class has different timing than others. Plan sponsors tend to want to put more capital into an asset class that's performing well. If the investment committee asks, "What's the return in this asset class for the last five years?" and you say, "Terrible," their typical response is "Don't invest in it." Conversely, if your answer is, "Great," they'll say, "Let's put more capital in it." Private investments have shown very high returns in the past couple of years. (Last year, ours returned 43%.) But increasing your investment in this asset class won't improve your pension fund's short-term performance. In fact, the investment you make today will show a negative return for the next two to three years.

The performance of limited partnership funds tends to follow a "J" curve, not unlike a hockey stick. Typically, you'll see negative returns for the first few years because management fees are so much higher than those for traditional investments. As already mentioned, a general partner's management fees and carried interest can account for about ten percentage points of a limited partnership fund's return. A fixed-income, index portfolio manager may cost you one basis point. If you hire an external advisor, you will have to pay between 50 and 100 basis points.

As the portfolio matures, returns start creeping up. Your first positive net cash flow should occur between years five and seven. It will take an additional five to seven years to generate your target returns consistently on an annual basis. If you expect a 15% net rate of return, you'll only reach that level between years ten through 15. You really need a long-term perspective.

You should also diversify in both venture capital and buyout funds. The 1980s illustrate why. In 1983, a booming IPO market provided wonderful venture capital returns. In 1984, money poured into these investments. The oversupply of capital created excessively high valuations for private companies: to this date, venture capital investments made in 1984 and 1985 have low single-digit returns. But for the diversified investor, these horrendous venture capital returns were offset by the performance of buyout funds: in the late 1980s, the buyout market collapsed. People who invested in buyouts at that time got very high returns.

To meet your primary goal of capturing overall market return, the best policy is to put in consistent dollars and make sure you have a presence in the market every year. From that base you can implement various value-added strategies to capture incremental returns.

TRENDS IN TODAY'S MARKET

The market can only absorb so much capital before it heats up to a level where everybody loses money. There is some concern today that the amount of capital to be invested is reaching a peak level again. Another concern is that too much capital is flowing to a relatively small number of venture capitalists and buyout specialists.

To some extent, this was inevitable. In picking a general partner, we all look for track record, for people who have worked together as a team for a long time and have consistent performance. Only the best survive, and they get bigger. But the venture capitalists who founded this industry are close to retirement age now and many younger people who worked under or with them are ready to move out on their own. We have to look for these changes, and support those people.

Venture capital and buyout limited partnerships are now a more mainstream investment than they were a decade ago and will probably become still more disciplined and institutionalized as they attract additional pension fund capital. But I don't think this asset class will ever be a truly mainstream investment. As the market becomes more efficient, the premium it pays over traditional investments will continue to narrow. Unless venture capital investors move into the international markets where there are opportunities to capture the inefficiencies of the market and generate high returns, domestic investors will eventually say, "It's not worth all this illiquidity, all this headache, for that premium." If that happens, of course, there'll be a shortage of capital again, setting the stage for higher future returns in the domestic market.

 S M A R T   P I L L S

- ➤ Take a long-term perspective. Don't expect short-term gains.

- ➤ Make an ongoing, annual commitment to the market.

- ➤ Diversify on two levels: invest in both venture capital and buyout partnerships and invest in many partnerships, but no more than are manageable.

- ➤ Create broad investment guidelines, but don't shoe-horn this asset class into traditional models and methodologies.

- ➤ Leave yourself enough flexibility to seize special opportunities, like the international markets — especially Asia.

- ➤ Plan day-to-day operations carefully to manage your time efficiently.

- ➤ Know the terms and conditions of partnership agreements inside and out — especially how they affect short and long-term returns to the limited partners.

- ➤ Use your general partners as a true resource; don't marry someone who just wants your money.

CHAPTER FIVE

MARKET RETURNS MINUS MARKET RISK:
"SKILL INVESTING" AT THE ROCKEFELLER FOUNDATION

David A. White

The Rockefeller Foundation, like many other institutions, finished off the 1980s in great form with higher returns than we had any right to expect. The operative question then became: "What will the 1990s bring?" Our answer: "Not as much." Market valuations at the beginning of the 1990s would make it highly unlikely that the strong returns of the previous decade could be repeated in this one. In our view, a balanced portfolio could produce an annual real return of 6%, in line with long-term historic results but significantly less than we had become accustomed to in the '80s.

MEETING OUR BASIC NEEDS:
DIVERSIFICATION THROUGH "SKILL INVESTING"

That would make it a challenge to achieve our basic objectives: to maintain the real value of the endowment and to spend 6% each year to "improve the well-being of mankind." We also realized that by working off a 6% base instead of a 10% base, as we had in the '80s, we were setting ourselves up for many unhappy periods when agonizing decisions to reduce grant programs would need to be made, even though we expected the low market volatility of the late 1980s and the early 1990s to continue. The answer clearly was increased participation in alternative asset classes — we already have nearly 20% of our assets in real estate, venture capital, junk bonds — to find additional sources of return and to protect the portfolio from capital market risk.

We decided to earmark an initial 5% of our overall portfolio, about $100 million, to what I call hedge fund, or "skill investing."[1] These are strategies that could produce a 6 to 8% real return through a variety of hedging techniques without capital market risk. In the case of stocks, that risk is stated as beta, or the price changes in your portfolio due to stock market fluctuations. With bonds, it's stated

---

[1] Because there is so much confusion about the definition of hedge fund investing, I prefer the latter term.

INVESTMENT MANAGEMENT AND CLIENT SERVICING
DEDICATED TO INSTITUTIONAL CLIENTS

EQUITY

FIXED-INCOME

INTERNATIONAL

CASH MANAGEMENT

For more information, please contact:

John E. Igneri
Senior Vice President
(212) 922-8420

The
Dreyfus
Trust Company
SM

as duration — or price movements in bonds due to the ups and downs of interest rates. If we could get beta and duration as close to zero as possible, we would be left with alpha: investment returns produced by skill alone, rather than from the fluctuations of the capital markets. Current economic theory holds that 80% of the returns produced by an active equity manager can be explained by market risk or beta, and only 20% by the manager's skill at stock picking. With our alternative strategy, we hoped to reverse those percentages.

"SKILL" STRATEGIES

How does one achieve the seemingly impossible — market returns without market risk? We chose two basic methods.

1. About 85% of our Alpha Fund portfolio is devoted to *arbitrage* strategies: buying a security in one market and selling it in another to take advantage of small price inefficiencies between the two, or buying the convertible securities of one company and shorting their common stock. This part of our portfolio is about evenly divided among fixed income, domestic equity and global equity arbitrage and we often use derivatives like futures to leverage the returns.

A good example of a strategy in this area is capital structure arbitrage where the manager buys the junk bonds of a troubled company and shorts the higher-rated bonds. If the company fails, both issues will go to zero and you've got a natural hedge; if the company succeeds, the junk bonds will perform much better, and that's what we're betting on. In fixed income arbitrage, a manager might buy ten-year Treasury bonds and short three-year Treasuries on a bet that the yield curve will flatten. In addition to leverage achieved by using futures, arbitrage strategies are also sometimes leveraged by financing positions with broker-dealers to achieve the 6% real return target.

2. The other 15% of our Alpha Fund portfolio is devoted to *traditional hedge funds* that pursue a more aggressive strategy: seeking out large inefficiencies in the market and pouncing on them. They might, for example, take a big position in one promising stock and short another company in the same industry. These managers will often incur market risk, or beta, because they're net long the market, but the key is they are not long forever. As long as they don't expose their portfolios to systematic beta, they qualify for our system. Moreover, because these hedge funds make up only 15% of our portfolio, the beta they do incur gets pretty well diversified away.

When you can achieve capital market returns without capital market risk, the impact on your overall portfolio is powerful. These returns are completely uncorrelated with the returns achieved by your other managers and lower overall volatility. A good Alpha Fund trader, for example, can make money in a bad market; a long stock picker will go down with the market. Sure, that stock picker might do well in a weak market at times, but that would be pretty hard to do in a year like 1974 or 1987. A really flexible Alpha manager, on the other hand, would be able to short the market. Our goal of an overall market return in this sector is obviously conservative. We could ramp up to more aggressive hedge funds with higher leverage or concentration and raise our return expectations, but we're trying to find another way to meet our 6% real return, long-term objective.

Eliminate "Dead Weight"

This strategy is powerful for another reason: we eliminate what I call the "dead weight" problem of most institutional portfolios. For example, typical long stock managers who are measured against an S&P 500 benchmark might not particularly like oil stocks. Yet they would have 6% of their assets invested in that sector because it comprises 8% of the S&P. But if you ask these managers about oil stocks, their knowledge is skimpy. Here they are, sitting on 6% of my money invested in something they know very little about simply because if they don't have 6% they run the risk of not tracking the S&P! Traditional institutional management creates a lot of this dead weight. Hedge fund managers, on the other hand, limit themselves to stocks that they've thoroughly researched and believe are going up — or down, if they've shorted them. Only their best ideas are in their portfolios.

In July 1993 we committed $100 million to "skill investing." We felt this was a large enough toe in the water to get a meaningful impact, and small enough so we weren't betting the ranch on it. To implement the strategy we chose 14 money management firms, all of them specialists in narrow niches. They could be big managers (John Merriweather has raised about $2 billion for fixed income arbitrage), but generally they are small —people who do one thing well. It's our belief that the so-called macro-hedge funds, the Steinhardts and Coopermans who got creamed in the first quarter of 1994, are into too many things to do any one thing well.

"Packaging": A Skill Investment Structure

We also structured this alternative differently from our portfolio of more traditional investments. We "packaged" our 14 managers into a separate multiple manager limited liability company (LLC), structured jointly by Rockefeller Foundation staff and manager Collins Associates. Collins created a separate account for us, a "fund of funds," which he runs for an overriding incentive fee. He serves, essentially, as the "manager" of our Alpha Fund, hiring most of the firms himself, monitoring their performance and treating each one as a separate "stock" or "bond." We chose this approach because we lacked the in-depth knowledge of most of the "skill" managers and Collins already had considerable experience, as well as the monitoring systems, in place. His firm is not alone; many others, such as Cambridge Associates, Evaluation Associates, or Tremont Partners now offer similar services and expertise in this area.

This "packaging" approach has another big advantage: it keeps us from falling into the trap of monitoring numbers month by month, or manager by manager. We're trying to deliver a "packaged" real return of 6% or better and we understand that there will be negative periods in any one deal. In fact, most of these strategies take much longer to work out because there is no dead weight and far less diversification. But the return of the multiple managers should be more stable.

Except for the traditional hedge funds, which are a much smaller piece of the Alpha Fund "pie," we divided our $100 million, or 5% of our total assets, pretty evenly among all 14 managers. Our reason: the track records in this "skill" sector are short, unstable and lack data and research. We feel pretty comfortable in predicting that we'll get a 6% return from owning stocks — we have 80 years of market history and a solid economic theory of why the stock market produces returns. In the alpha sector, returns are much harder to predict; there isn't even a theory of where they come from except skill. As a result, we couldn't be confident that one strategy would be more successful over the long run than another.

In fact, these realities pretty much determined our approach to the Foundation committee as we sought approval for our "skill investing" strategy. The debate in committee lasted for nearly a year and was largely conceptual. We didn't invite any hedge fund managers, advisors or consultants to the committee meetings to

apply their strong persuasive powers; I presented the pros and cons of the "skill investing" concept based on extensive conversations I'd had with both money managers and consultants. I give the trustees great credit; this was a big departure from the capital markets strategy that had served us so well in the 1980s. But they did have some building blocks on which to base their decision: the Foundation had already undertaken a very small controlled experiment with hedging and currency strategies and it had worked. We could show the trustees real time and real money, rather than have some smart mouth come in and say "I did 30% last year."

A Tip

My biggest piece of advice for other sponsors considering "skill investing" is: get deep into the business terms of each deal and negotiate hard. The big challenge to people on my side of the table is to structure these deals with more visibility, or transparency. You want to see everything, just as you do with your traditional long stock and bond managers, and that is difficult. In the alpha sector, you have to enter a partnership; your funds are commingled with other investors and the managing partner tends to be noncommunicative. You have to wait to get a report, you can't look into the portfolio, you often have an opportunity to move out only once a year. The fees are high — double or triple the average long fee — and the structures are impenetrable because the manager is obviously rationing his skills. Here are some terms we try to negotiate — not always, I might say, with complete success.

Target Negotiating Terms

1. *Strict limits on assets under management*: In view of the high manager fees, your manager should limit his number of clients; high assets under management usually limit returns.

2. *Share income from outside businesses*: We don't want our managers to get rich just because they're using our capital to enter ancillary businesses. And if they do so, we want to share in the fees. If, for example, a manager earns a high fee for serving on a creditor's committee, we want it all to be split in the deal. This is a big point of contention with some managers.

3. *Incentive structures to control risk*: We try to keep our incentive fees to 15 to 20% of profits, which is low. Many managers want 30%. But we also want to structure those fees to keep our managers from taking too much, or too little, risk. We try to cap returns: the manager earns no fee after a return of 25% has been earned on our money. That's enough for us; we don't want to encourage unlimited risk to get unlimited returns. Conversely, we insist that our managers get no fees until they've earned a 10% return for us, an incentive to make them seek returns and not just sit on our money.

4. *Separate accounts*: If we have enough money with a manager — the threshold is generally about $20 million — we ask for a separate account. This is the key to greater transparency and the ability to terminate the manager at will which we demand as well. We also ask that a limited liability company own the account — to limit our own liability if the manager goes bankrupt — and that the manager provide his own Errors and Omissions insurance.

Our "Skill Investing" Track Record

How has the structure worked so far? In our first year of "skill investing" we've achieved our objective of 6% to 8% real return without capital market risk, excluding one bad experience. One of our managers was David Askin, the mortgage arbitrageur who got caught in a liquidity bind, departed from his hedging strategies and went bankrupt. But the Askin debacle taught us an important lesson: we need more controls and better systematic monitoring. We're now installing an extra layer of due diligence, working with our brokers to see if we can get portfolios monitored on a regular basis, and scheduling many more meetings with our managers. We also plan to add staff to provide a chance for someone else to say "No."

 S M A R T   P I L L S

- ➤ Don't confuse skill and luck. While their track records may be impressive, hedge fund managers have had an easy time making money brainlessly during the bull markets of the last few years. You could have matched their performance simply by buying the BIG Salomon bond index and leveraging it 5 to 1 with CFTC[2] settled futures.

- ➤ Don't be over-confident. This is an area where you can never get enough information. The numbers are very unstable and track records are short. You should never let your confidence in one firm or strategy dominate your decision-making process.

- ➤ Be patient. In order to get alpha, you have to give managers a long time frame. These strategies can be very volatile in the short run and people with queasy stomachs shouldn't be players in this game.

- ➤ Look for high turnover. Make sure a manager's record is not based on one or two big bets; it's hard to replicate that going forward. Conversely, a high-turnover, high-frequency betting strategy gives you statistical confidence that there is real skill behind the reported results. And you can afford it; transaction costs are much lower in the "skill" area.

---

[2] Commodities Futures Trading Commission

CHAPTER SIX

DUPONT'S INVESTMENT LENS: S.O.S. FOR DISTRESSED DEBT

Carmen J. Gigliotti

Many investors approach alternative assets from an asset allocation perspective and look for portfolio diversification and risk reduction in addition to total return. At DuPont, we take a somewhat different approach: to us, return is king.

As a result, our approach to alternative asset investing is best described as opportunistic. *Our entire program is rooted in the premise that we want to be only in those areas that provide us with opportunities to add to the total return of the pension fund.* We don't want to be exposed across the market and see only an average return for the asset class.

This strategy was really developed when DuPont began to beef up its alternative asset investing program back in the mid- to late 1980s. Although the pension fund had been in alternative assets since the 1970s, it had never been a concerted, proactive effort. But when Tom Croft and the other managers here at the time decided to make alternative assets a strategically important part of DuPont's portfolio, they didn't want simply to jump into it. In fact, they spent a lot of time just thinking about the most productive way we should approach the area.

Not surprisingly, when a final decision was made, DuPont decided to consider alternative assets — which we define as everything outside the liquid, public markets — in the same way we approach the rest of our portfolio. In our public investing, we are *value investors*, using a number of different strategies to identify investment opportunities—from dividend discount models to low price to earnings and low price to book value ratios.

FINDING OPPORTUNITIES FOR VALUE INVESTING

We looked for a way we could bring that value orientation to our alternative investing and identify attractive market sectors or strategies and invest in them. Generally, our goal was to find investments where we could earn excess returns over the liquid public markets. The question that remained was whether we could identify objective, quantifiable criteria for such a value investing program in the same way we had developed a value investment methodology for our public portfolio.

CHECKING OUT YOUR VENTURE CAPITAL PARTNER

What we ended up with was a set of criteria that looks for the following in an investment opportunity: an inefficient market, a supply-demand imbalance in the capitalization of a market sector, and fund managers with a disciplined approach to their investment program.

Looking at the market through those filters led us to de-emphasize real estate in the mid-1980s. At the time we made a very conscious decision to stay away from real estate assets because we felt we were in a deflationary environment and, while there was a supply-demand imbalance in the market's capitalization, it was working the wrong way. There was too much money in the market and not enough demand for it. Obviously, given the ensuing turmoil in the real estate market, that call turned out to be prescient.

Applying those same measures now, *we are cautious about* large LBO funds — an area that has seen a lot of money raised recently without any apparent corresponding increase in demand for LBO equity financing — and venture capital. For a long time, there was significant excess capital in the venture capital market. That in turn drove up valuations in a classic supply-demand imbalance scenario and diluted returns on the back side. Now that situation seems to have corrected itself but we still don't like venture capital. We believe that the market is small; it's easy for investors to make mistakes due to increased investment interest. Venture capital simply is not compelling when viewed through our investment lens. Venture capital investing takes a long time and we're not convinced that the returns are worth the wait.

Ironically, the same value investing criteria that drove us away from real estate compelled us to give real estate a second look in 1991. There's still considerable distress in that sector creating some severe market inefficiencies and while some money has been raised to invest in the real estate area, it is far from enough to clean up the mess out there. Accordingly, real estate is an area we like today.

Our investment philosophy also led us into the distressed debt sector several years ago, a bet which also has proven to be a good one. At the time, that asset class met all of our investment criteria. First, the market for distressed companies is inherently inefficient. Generally, bankruptcy is an area that many people simply don't like and won't touch. They don't understand it. It takes a lot of time and work to get a company through bankruptcy. And, there's an important perception problem: most companies won't want to buy a company out of bankruptcy because of the anticipated negative reaction from shareholders, although they're more than happy to buy the same company after it's been cleaned up a bit.

Second, there was a tremendous supply-demand imbalance. After almost a decade of LBO feeding frenzy activity, literally hundreds of companies were overburdened with debt that they could service only if they met pie-in-the-sky earnings projections. With the economy tipping into recession, it wasn't hard to see what was coming: within months the bankruptcy pipeline would be stuffed, ensuring a healthy demand for capital. At the same time, debt for these companies could be had on the cheap. Tainted by scandal and stigmatized by the public's perception that they were high risk, no-win investments, high-yield junk bonds were a screaming "buy" for a very simple reason: there was no supply of capital for these companies.

As always, hindsight is 20-20 vision and retrospect makes it easy to see why the distressed debt area was a good investment several years ago. But we are pleased with the key to our investment methodology: our evaluation of market conditions led us into the distressed debt area before it became red hot and overplayed. We have to be pro-active when we uncover these market opportunities and seek appropriate partners. I think the key, however, is to be receptive and have the market knowledge to recognize good opportunities when they come in. After all, with more than $14 billion in capital, DuPont is on almost everyone's fundraising short list.

I should also note that distressed debt opportunities are point-in-time phenomena; they inevitably pass. With virtually all the major bankruptcies and out-of-chapter restructurings complete, distressed debt is not as attractive an area as it used to be. While we still have money in the distressed debt sector, most of that money going forward will probably be put to work in the senior debt sector with companies that do not have access to the public debt market, an area that still has a way to go before its returns are fully tapped.

OUR INVESTMENT PROCESS

Of course, identifying sectors for strategic emphasis in our portfolio is only the first step in our investment process. We didn't follow our decision to invest in distressed debt by putting money in the first three firms we could find pursuing that investment strategy.

After identifying an attractive opportunity, we look for someone who can execute it for us. *To us, that means assessing experience.* The issue of experience always puts the alternative asset investor in a quandary. On the one hand, you can become very narrow in your investment focus if you say you won't ever invest in a first-time fund. On the other hand, you want to put your money with someone who knows what they're doing. It's a real chicken-and-egg situation.

The bottom line is that we like to see someone with a track record and we want to see groups that have worked together as a team. I should note, however, that the

LOOKING TO IMPROVE YOUR STOCK/BOND PORTFOLIO?

Enhanced Returns

Reduced Risk

Global Opportunities

Professional Management

{ AND WE'RE NOT EVEN TO THE BEST PART YET. }

The best part is, **Managed Futures** can easily add desired portfolio diversification in one investment.

One, the possibility of enhanced returns exists since Managed Futures are not correlated with stocks or bonds. Because you can easily take long or short futures positions, you have the ability to benefit in bull or bear markets. **Two**, by further diversifying your portfolio, it is possible to reduce overall portfolio risk. **Three**, with the global products available in the futures markets, you have the

Managed Futures

opportunity for international exposure. And **four**, currently more than $22 billion is being managed by registered Commodity Trading Advisors.

Enhanced returns, diversification, globalization and professional management. All possible in a single addition to your stock and bond portfolio.

Managed Futures. To find out more about this investment, call 1-800-THE-CBOT ext. 7510, or 1-312-435-3558 ext. 7510 to receive a complimentary copy of the CBOT's managed futures brochure.

⊚ **Chicago Board of Trade**

team experience doesn't always have to be in the area the fund managers want to exploit. In fact, if it's a truly novel strategy, there may not be anyone out there with directly relevant experience. But what we do want to see is the expertise and experience that demonstrate the capability to carry out investment strategy.

I also mentioned discipline as a key criteria in our value investing strategy. We look for that discipline in the manager rather than in the markets themselves. We want to make sure these managers are going to make the investments and exploit the opportunity the way they say they will. We want to see certain parameters in the investment process and people who say: "We won't pay more than x for these types of assets." We don't want to invest with people who are going to be overly attracted to a sexy opportunity; we prefer a more nuts and bolts approach.

As part of that discipline, we want to see focus as well. A lot of institutional investors don't utilize industry-specific funds because they believe they're too risky. I believe just the opposite is true. I want to see a group that's focused 100% on their sector of the market. In any case, if you are trying to diversify away your risk, it should be done at the portfolio level.

We saw all of these elements in the three fund managers we invested with in the distressed debt area. Additionally, they came to us with a very realistic, very conservative approach. They gave us a terrific downside analysis, focusing on liquidation value or the market value of the going concern. To us, that emphasized their value orientation.

The other major issue we pay attention to in our due diligence process is commonality of interest. Commonality of interest is crucial to us. We don't want to participate in funds where the general partner puts little or nothing in and gets huge management and transaction fees. We want them to be properly incented so that if we make money, they make money and if we lose, they lose too.

One way of ensuring that the interests of the general partner and the limited partner coincide is to insist on a significant capital contribution by the fund manager. There may be no better way of committing the fund manager to the investing program than by putting his or her own money at risk. In short, fund managers should be willing to put their money where their mouths are.

Of course, "significant" is a nebulous term. Our rule of thumb is usually on the order of 30%: we want a substantial portion of the fund's capital to come from the manager or we expect the manager to put up a significant percentage of his or her net worth.

The other primary way to ensure commonality of interest is through the proper fee structure. First, the management fee should be set to the proper level. *We really focus on management fees as a reimbursement tool, not as a profit center.* The fund manager should not get his or her return from the management fee.

Another important aspect of the fee structure is the carried interest. Generally, we stick to the standard 20% carry seen in performance management structures. But we also look for performance hurdles. The bottom line is that we don't want the general partner to get their carried interest early; we don't care if they make a significant profit as long as we realize above-average returns.

As for other structural matters, we usually make sure that we have an ability to terminate the investment process. A lot of funds in the 1980s were structured with no money from the general partners and no way for the limited partners to stop the managers from running amok. To me, that's a bad structure. We usually ask for provisions that enable us to throw out the manager and we think that's perfectly reasonable. After all, its mostly our money.

Last but not least, there's our standard due diligence fare including background checks, information on previous deals and references. That end of the process is fairly straightforward with most calls going out to lawyers, accountants and previous co-investors.

LOOKING BACKWARD, AND FORWARD

So far, our approach to the asset class is paying off. Our alternative investment portfolio as a whole has yielded returns in the mid-teens in the recent past and we've netted returns of well over 20% on our distressed debt portfolio. Looking ahead, we hope to do more of the same although I expect that our alternative portfolio will see returns in the high teens in the coming years.

At the same time, our expectations on the liquid public markets have ratcheted down and I don't think we'll see much more than single digits to 10% on domestic public equities in the balance of the '90s. With that kind of return differential, we could easily see ourselves stepping up our activity in the alternative area, perhaps approaching our cap on the asset class.

Because of our opportunistic investment focus, it's difficult to say where we'll be putting that money. I mentioned that we like real estate right now, and I'd like to see us do more direct investing, probably in a co-investment role with our general partners. As for the rest, we'll have to see if our investment lens really has 20-20 vision.

 S M A R T   P I L L S

➤ Look for value areas in the alternative asset arena, particularly where there is a supply-demand imbalance in capital availability.

➤ Look for inefficient markets where your fund managers enjoy some type of advantage.

➤ Insist on commonality of interest. It's crucial.

➤ Find fund managers who are focused. Don't get hung up on portfolio diversification.

➤ Stress investment discipline.

➤ Make sure you have the ability to terminate the investment process. You should be able to fire a bad manager.

CHAPTER SEVEN

PRUDENCE FIRST:
PENNSYLVANIA'S ETI RISK AND RETURN MANDATE

Erica C. Bushner

Economically Targeted Investments (ETIs) within the Pennsylvania State Employes' Retirement System portfolio mean venture capital investments with a geographical focus on the Commonwealth of Pennsylvania. It's important to add, however, that even though exposure to Pennsylvania is a significant component of our venture capital investing, the program's primary function is to enhance return and diversify investment risk within the total pension fund.

That caveat is worth emphasizing because I believe that considering risk and return is of foremost importance in crafting a successful ETI or geographically targeted venture investment program. If you slam-dunk geographically or socially oriented investments into a portfolio without this primary focus on risk and return, the program flounders and eventually gets cut off — and nobody benefits. In a successful ETI program, in fact, the geographic or social target is really a kind of ancillary benefit.

Despite our geographic bent, we don't limit our investments to Pennsylvania venture capital funds. We also invest as well in regional and national funds that have a history of making Pennsylvania investments. There's a double benefit to this broader approach: investing in regional and national funds gives us greater diversification and, at the same time, helps attract out-of-state capital to Pennsylvania. In 1990, for example, we invested $3 million in Grotech Partners, a Maryland-based regional fund capitalized at $51 million. Grotech Partners made a handful of Pennsylvania investments that totaled more than $3 million. In effect, we used the power of leverage: we got more bang for our buck than we would have with a Pennsylvania-domiciled partnership that invested one-third to one-half its capital here.

Another advantage to this strategy is that regional and national funds bring expertise as well as capital to the companies they invest in. Obviously, Pennsylvania venture capital funds have expertise, too. But the national and regional funds may have a wider perspective and better access to capital nationwide.

By law we can now invest up to 2% of the total fund's book value in this asset

T-BOND FUTURES AND OPTIONS

10-YEAR T-NOTE FUTURES AND OPTIONS

5-YEAR T-NOTE FUTURES AND OPTIONS

2-YEAR T-NOTE FUTURES AND OPTIONS

30-DAY FED FUND FUTURES

MUNI-BOND FUTURES AND OPTIONS

CANADIAN GOVERNMENT BOND FUTURES AND OPTIONS

EXTENDED HOURS FOR EXTENDED YIELD CURVE OPPORTUNITY

Starting in September, you can trade financial futures and options contracts between 2:30 and 4:30 p.m. Chicago time, while the cash market is still open. For additional information on the Project A® trading system, call 1-800-THE-CBOT, ext. 8065, or 1-312-435-3558, ext. 8065.*

Pending CFTC approval.

Chicago Board of Trade

class. Currently, we have approximately $260 million committed to 22 venture capital partnerships. To balance out our venture capital investments, since 1988 we have also invested in other types of private equity deals such as buyouts. This second program, which we call alternative investments, has no geographic component and also represents 2% of total fund assets; we can invest 4% of the total fund in private equities.

The IPO market has been very attractive in the past couple of years, while public market returns are projected to be less attractive in this decade than in the past. The result is that people who were spooked in the late 1980s are now coming back into private equities. The danger is that once this market is too crowded and managers are flush with cash, they may start putting it out at higher multiples.

We've tried to avoid the crowd that has flocked to late-stage venture capital. Starting this year, we invested in a large fund with an early stage component. We're also looking at another fund that's a niche player, small enough so it won't attract the mega public and corporate funds but large enough to be of institutional quality. And although at some future date we may bump up our allocation in the private equity area, we may soon go to the sidelines for a while.

Our target return for all private equity investments is a net 14% over a ten-year horizon, or about 5% over what we can expect on the public equity side. Our best-performing fund right now has a 33% return. Of course, we've also had some lackluster funds, but on a total portfolio basis we haven't had many disasters. In fact, based on our performance, the legislature in 1990 increased our venture capital allocation from 1% to the current 2% of fund assets; at the same time, we also increased our alternative investment program from 1% to 2%.

Our ETI program has evolved and broadened in several ways since its inception in 1985. Our original mandate from the legislature was to make venture capital investments "that enhance the general welfare of the Commonwealth of Pennsylvania through economic development, and meet standards of prudence." The 1994 law simply directs us to make venture capital investments that, in the judgment of the board of trustees, "will enhance the general welfare of the Commonwealth and its citizens, and meet standards of prudence," and omits the phrase "economic development."

Before 1989, we invested only in Pennsylvania-domiciled venture capital partnerships and we wanted language that said they would make their best efforts to invest a sizable portion of their money in Pennsylvania. But we saw early on that insisting that they focus exclusively on in-state investments might invite syndication risk: Pennsylvania partnerships all looking for deals in the state could easily wind up taking a piece of the same investment. If you're in five partnerships that invest in the same deal, your return is the same but your risk is bigger. Your return can also be diminished by the fact that competing funds in the same geographic area could bid up the price ultimately paid for the portfolio investment.

If you're too geographically restrictive, you also forgo good investment opportunities. For example, NEPA Ventures, a Pennsylvania-domiciled seed fund we invested in during 1985, had all its deals in Pennsylvania except one. But that deal, a California investment made in conjunction with a West Coast partnership, was one of its most successful. The company went IPO and should be a winner.

In the last eighteen months, we have invested in two national funds. We look for regional and national funds with a history of Pennsylvania investing that we can expect will look at Pennsylvania deals in the future. But it's a mistake to make ETIs the overriding objective; if you do, corporate pension funds will be scared off. That's a lose/lose situation. It's much better to invest in a larger fund and be a limited partner in a group that invests in Pennsylvania.

One of the best ways to present this type of strategy to your board of trustees is through an Annual Investment Plan. We do an annual plan that involves all the fund's asset managers and consultants. We start with an inflation assumption and build in what we think every asset class will earn. It's a chance to show the board the opportunities we feel are out there, what we think we should avoid right now and why a program is justified in going forward. I used our Annual Investment Plan in 1989 and 1990 as opportunities to explain why diversifying our portfolio through regional and national funds was a win/win strategy.

INPUT FROM IN-HOUSE STAFF AND CONSULTANTS

We have a two-person staff solely dedicated to managing the 4% of the fund invested in private equities. We also use Cambridge Associates as a consultant. They have an extensive database and analytical ability that keeps me abreast of what's going on in the marketplace. A discretionary consultant would make more sense for a smaller fund that lacks a knowledgeable staff but wants to get into this market without paying the fees associated with a fund of funds.

A discretionary consultant will find and recommend partnerships in which to invest whatever percentage of your assets you want to allocate to private equity investments. If you're willing to do the record-keeping you save money, but a consultant's fund of funds gives you one nice neat report and frees you from tons of paperwork. If you have staff that know their stuff, a discretionary advisor doesn't make sense — the advisor and staff start tripping over each other.

PICKING VENTURE CAPITAL PARTNERSHIPS

We keep an active deal log of venture capital opportunities. Everyone knows we're in the marketplace looking for partnerships and we get every offering memorandum. We give each one a brief review. If it fits our annual investment policy, we take a closer look. We may call the group, ask them to come in and meet with us. We'll ask Cambridge for its thoughts on a fund. In this way, we develop a short list. If it's a group we really like and our consultant likes, we'll have more meetings.

At this point, a meeting with the partnership in their office is mandatory. The chief investment officer may join the private equity investment staff for a full day as part of this due diligence. We want to meet everybody from the board room to the mail room. We want to know: "Is it an environment that encourages smart thinking?" "Is it a monarchy or truly a partnership with a team vision?"

If we're still interested, I'll send them a standard three-to-four page questionnaire to assemble the appropriate numbers and determine their internal rate of return. I want to see cash in/cash out distributions, net of fees and net of partner's carried interest. If they have unrealized gains, I want to pick through the terminal value, see what they're holding it at and evaluate what it's worth. They send a copy of their response to our consultant. Although Cambridge has its own

From every
investment field....

...We'll assemble the right products <u>for you</u>

At MetLife, we translate extensive investment capabilities into customized solutions. Drawing upon the vast resources of MetLife and its family of investment management subsidiaries, specialists experienced with Foundation & Endowments will work with you to create a tailored investment program to meet your investment management needs.

MetLife, with $93 billion under management for retirement plans and other institutional clients, offers an unsurpassed array of investment capabilities*, including:

- Actively Managed Domestic and International Equity and Fixed Income

- Passively Managed Equity and Fixed Income

- Structured Fixed Income

- Institutional Real Estate

In appropriate situations, MetLife offers certain of these capabilities on a guaranteed basis.

Isn't it time you put the resources of MetLife to work for you?

For further information, contact:
HARVEY M. YOUNG, Senior Vice President
Telephone (212) 578-6287

✻ **MetLife**®

questionnaire process, and does its own due diligence independent of ours, relying on a consultant doesn't absolve you from doing your own homework.

THE MAGIC NUMBER: 40 DOCUMENTED DUE DILIGENCE CALLS

When we do our due diligence, we always try to make a minimum of 40 documented phone calls — that's our magic number. We check personal references, other venture capitalists, and private equity managers, senior lenders, mezzanine lenders, all who have done deals with them. If the due diligence comes up clean, staff and consultant jointly recommend to the board of trustees that they interview the firm. It's up to the candidate to present itself to the board before it makes the final decision.

We take a very active role in monitoring the partnerships we invest in. We always try to secure seats on the valuation advisory board or on the valuation committee. We currently serve on about 19 such boards in the venture capital area. Private equity valuation committees are almost a form of corporate governance. You get a lot of details on the companies, and you're recommending and blessing the values that the general partners propose — values that will affect everyone's return. If I can't secure a seat, I want to know who of my peers is on the board to be sure we have good coverage.

On the venture capital side, we also monitor the extent of Pennsylvania investments. We have a database that tracks when investments are made, their cost, value, and location. Once a year, we ask all our venture capital managers for a report listing their Pennsylvania holdings with estimated number of employees, estimated payroll for the coming year, capital commitments from out-of-state, and follow-on commitments. We report all this to the board.

ADVICE TO NEWCOMERS

Read your documents thoroughly. Check side letters, as well. We make sure we see every side letter the partners agree to. If there are any social or geographical investing criteria they've agreed to — special considerations, best efforts — they'll show up in side letters. Once you sign on the dotted line, you've basically got a ten to 13-year marriage contract. In the courtship phase everybody loves everybody. Once the honeymoon is over, things can change.

Venture capital investors enjoy a very strong network: we talk among ourselves. At times we call each other during the negotiation process. Sometimes a general partner says, "Nobody else asked for that," and in fact, everybody did and what's more, we all know it. As a limited partner, if you find something in the documents you don't understand, call one of your peers and ask about it.

Be sure to get key man provisions: a change in personnel could affect your investment. I remember one situation in which we negotiated a key man provision because we wanted to be sure that at least one of two key people would stay. We expected the senior of the two would leave. As it turned out, it was the junior person who left, but at least our provision roped in the senior guy for the life of the partnership. A key man provision should kick in something specific — enable you to stop funding, for example, or give you the ability to approve someone new.

You can't make unreasonable demands when you negotiate this prenuptial agreement. A partnership is a long-term relationship that you shouldn't expect to get out of easily. No general partner wants capricious investors, but if the strategy isn't working and a majority of the partners wants to call it quits, they should be able to get a no-fault divorce.

PRACTICAL CONSIDERATIONS

If you want to reach a 2% investment target over a five-year period, you need a game plan to get there. *I think it's very important to try to dollar average into the market*, so you'll be exposed to all conditions each year. We also take cash flow into account. On average, it takes between four and five years for partners to draw capital down; and it takes another couple of years for an investment to mature. Of the $257.5 million we had committed as of March 1994, for example, partners have only drawn down $111 million and we've received $54 million.

As a result of these cash flow considerations, our rule of thumb is to over-allocate by at least 135%. If you don't do that, you don't get to your target, because the capital isn't all drawn down on day one.

HOT TOPICS: DIRECT INVESTING AND CO-INVESTING

Direct investing and co-investing are hot topics. We are not set up for direct investing, which means sourcing your own deals. In fact, I admit to some skepticism about whether any pension fund is set up for it. If you're working for a venture capital or private equity partnership, you have a competitive salary, big upside potential and the resources to source your own deals. Conversely, on both the public and corporate pension side you don't necessarily have that big upside motivation. Your upside is capped — but if you find and invest in a deal that turns sour, your downside is unlimited. In essence, when plan sponsors do direct investing, blame for a bad deal cannot be shifted to a group of general partners, nor can the bad returns be buried in a diverse group of partnership investments.

I think co-investing, where you invest on an equal basis with a general partner who leads you to deals, works better on the corporate side than on the public pension side. We aren't structured for it, but for a corporate fund it can be an excellent strategy. Similarly, I think we're a couple of years behind our corporate counterparts when it comes to investing in global private equity funds. There's the issue of travel, for example. It's no problem to travel internationally if you have branches all over the world. For a pension fund, it can be an issue.

THE FUTURE

One of the many unresolved issues raised by the hot IPO market of the past couple of years is whether a venture capital partnership should own stock. I think some general partners are attracted to the fact that owning public stock lets them sit on the boards of public companies. My own view is that once a partnership has public stock, they should get rid of it in a prudent manner as soon as possible. General partners aren't stock managers or small-cap experts — public stock management should be left to the post-venture capital managers.

Some pension funds want partners to distribute the stock. That's not our position. We give the general partner cash and, in our view, a round trip is embedded in the management fee: we want cash back. I measure returns on a cash-in and cash-out basis. If a partner gives stock back, he has uncoupled the performance. Then you've only got three quarters of the story and the last quarter is buried with someone at the pension fund who handles public equities.

My suggestion is that partners solve this problem by employing post-venture capital consultants to manage any public stock they own with orders to sell it as profitably as possible. Venture capital and private equity partners use consultants all the time — health care and environmental experts, personality consultants — when companies are looking for a new CEO. Multiple consultant fees are embedded in the general partner's management fee. I think they should contract out this post-venture service, and provide for it as part of their management fee.

As non-traditional investing expands during the rest of the decade, I'm confident that issues like these will be discussed and considered among a wider circle of pension managers who become more and more outspoken alternative investors.

 S M A R T   P I L L S

➤ In selecting ETI investments, focus first on risk and return or you won't achieve your investment goals or your geographic and/or social objectives.

➤ Don't restrict partnerships to your own ETI objectives so narrowly that you scare off other potential investors.

➤ Use an Annual Investment Plan to educate your board about alternative investments and broaden your ETI strategy.

➤ Choose a consultant whose abilities will complement, not duplicate, your own; but no matter how much you rely on a consultant, don't stop doing your own homework.

➤ Negotiate agreements that are fair to both you and your partners. Don't draw up an agreement that precludes the possibility of a no-fault divorce if things don't work out.

➤ Get seats on your partnerships' valuation advisory boards: it's a great way to monitor the portfolio.

THE DIFFERENCE BETWEEN EXPLORING ON YOUR OWN AND FOLLOWING A GUIDE IN THE ALTERNATIVE INVESTMENT MARKETPLACE.

The alternative investment market is familiar terrain for us. In fact, for more than 13 years, the Private Equity Group at Merrill Lynch has been offering institutional equity funds in all areas of alternative investments—from the buyout arena to emerging markets. And because of our global reach and institutional placement expertise, we have attracted exceptionally qualified fund sponsors as clients. As a result, investors in the funds we have offered have reaped tremendous returns.

Merrill Lynch not only offers you the best quality product available, we make your selection and closing process more efficient. We perform thorough due diligence and only bring funds to market after we have carefully evaluated the sponsor and thoroughly analyzed its track record. Additionally, since we are always aware of the latest market terms, we offer products that have the characteristics and structure demanded most by investors.

We know our way around. And we can guide you to the most exceptional opportunities. That's why exploring the alternative investment market with the aid of an experienced guide can make a difference for your pension fund.

The difference is Merrill Lynch.

Merrill Lynch

A tradition of trust.

CHAPTER
EIGHT

PUSHING THE INNOVATION ENVELOPE:
SAN DIEGO'S MANAGED FUTURES PROGRAM

Richard N. Rose

I n March 1994, the San Diego County Employees' Retirement Association began trading managed futures. We believe this managed futures investment program will enhance the fund's total return and, at the same time, reduce its overall volatility. Although our initial allocation is $45 million— only 2% of the fund — over the long haul, I don't think it makes sense to have so little of the fund committed to any one asset class. We'll re-evaluate the managed futures program in a year or so, and either decide that it hasn't worked or increase our allocation. If it works as well as we expect, I anticipate we'll increase our allocation to about 5% of the fund.

Simply stated, a managed futures program is a global investment strategy in which a fund actively trades futures contracts in a myriad of markets and instruments. In our program, for example, we take both long and short positions in some 50 to 60 different markets. These include the financial markets where we trade futures contracts in interest rates, currencies, global stock indexes, and commodities markets for metals, energies, and agricultural products.

The initiation of our program caps three years spent studying this asset class. In the course of our research, we found that traditional consultants don't bring a lot to the table in this area. They've been slow to embrace managed futures as a viable investing strategy. In our case, we were lucky to have been introduced to managed futures in 1989 by Dave Love, a former member of our board, who was president of Monmouth Capital Management, a manager specializing in managed futures. Dave has remained close to our subsequent boards and was the first person to discuss this asset class with our administrator and board members.

I advise others who want to learn about managed futures to attend conferences such as those sponsored by the Chicago Mercantile Exchange, the Chicago Board of Trade and the Managed Futures Association, and talk to peers who've had experience with this asset class rather than turn to traditional consultants for guidance. I also strongly recommend reading **Managed Futures and Their Role in Investment Portfolios** by Don Chance.[1] I wish it had been available a few years ago.

---

[1] Research Foundation of the Institute of Chartered Financial Analysts, April, 1994.

When I was introduced to this asset class, my first question was, "Where are the returns coming from?" I thought: "Commodities and currencies are objects —there's no value creation there." There are two schools of thought about the source of the returns. One is that producers — farmers, energy producers, and others — pay a premium to transfer risk in the futures market so they can have more predictable revenue streams.

In this view, one is simply moving further out on the securities market line and receiving a higher expected return for a higher level of risk. The other is that returns are added as a result of managers' trading skill. These two theories aren't mutually exclusive, of course; in fact, we concluded there's much truth in both of them.

In several respects, investing in a managed futures program is almost the opposite of investing in traditional asset classes. A managed futures program requires very active trading, for example, instead of a passive buy and hold approach. It also involves taking both long and short positions — a tough concept to accept for anyone used to a traditional program where going short is almost sacrilegious.

But managed futures is an appealing investment strategy precisely because it provides a symmetry that doesn't exist in traditional investments. Traditional investing is fundamentally asymmetrical: you take one position, and it's a long position. If the S&P 500 is down and you have an active equity manager who is down less than the index, he's viewed as doing his job. His performance is always based on a long benchmark. But if that same investment manager had the ability to take a symmetrical, short position, as he does in managed futures, you can expect that if the S&P 500 is down, he might be up.

In studying managed futures, we looked at the BARRA-MLM, an index of managed futures and at its historical relationship to the MAR index, a composite of managed accounts. The MLM is a constructed index which replicates a simple futures trading strategy in a host of markets by taking long and short positions. The MAR index is the actual returns of a number of pool operators and commodity trading advisors.

We looked at the relationship of these two indexes going back about 12 years. We also looked at the correlation of their return streams with our existing portfolio. We found that while the indexes were inherently very volatile, because they were slightly negatively correlated with our existing portfolio, when we introduced even a small exposure to the portfolio, we reduced its overall volatility. We also found that over the period we studied, the longest time for which data was available, the indexes had a historical annualized return well in excess of our portfolio as it was actually constructed.

Our study introduced 2% of the BARRA-MLM index into the past ten years of our existing portfolio. The result was an increase in our annualized return from 11.86 to 12.03%, and a reduction of our standard deviation from 8.45 to 8.30%. The correlation of the index to the portfolio was negative at .02%. As you can imagine, when we feed this into our optimizer, it says "Give me more, give me more."

We demonstrated to our board of trustees that the standard deviation of our portfolio for the ten-year period we looked at was 8.45, and the standard deviation for managed futures over that same period was 16.93. They were surprised that because of the powerful diversifying effect of the slightly negative correlation, when we exposed our portfolio to managed futures we lowered its volatility. That's what modern portfolio theory teaches us about the effect of low or negative correlation: the right mix of uncorrelated assets optimizes your return per unit of risk. What our study revealed is an extension of the same concept, but we're not used to seeing it in such dramatic terms.

Because managed futures exposure reduces the portfolio's overall volatility, it increases the investment manager's overall flexibility. If we were comfortable with the fund's overall deviation before we put in managed futures, for example, adding managed futures would let us ratchet up something else in the fund, bringing us back to our original deviation. We could increase our investment in another potentially high return asset class like small-cap stocks, convertible bonds, or high yield bonds.

I think there are two reasons, both benefits, why exposure to managed futures indexes increased the portfolio's overall return. One is that a managed futures strategy allows you to take short positions. During a phase when stocks are doing poorly, your managed futures program potentially could take a short position in stock index futures and perform well. The second is that managed futures introduces commodities. If you look at a long position in the Goldman Sachs Commodity Index, you'll see that the index performs very well during periods of high inflation which is exactly when other, traditional, asset classes have a hard time. Gold, a traditional hedge against inflation, is one of those commodities, of course. Clearly there are a lot of good tactical reasons to invest in this asset class in the 1990s, perhaps a period of lower interest rates with the potential for inflationary periods.

We expect our program's return over time to be about 1.5 to 2 times the S&P 500, and about 1.5 to 2 times the S&P's standard deviation. I think a managed futures program can achieve a sustained, annualized return of 15% to 25%, depending on how you structure it and how much volatility you're prepared to bear. I view managed futures as a total return strategy: if the S&P 500 is down, I don't expect managed futures to be down. I expect one-, two-, and three-year returns to be positive, regardless of what's going on in other markets.

MASTERING THE COMFORT CURVE: SETTING UP A PROGRAM

For trustees, the steepest learning curve in this asset class may be a comfort curve. Accepting the ideas of being short, doing 1,000 trades a day or owning pork bellies is a major hurdle. But there are more mundane barriers to overcome as well, namely the nuts and bolts of setting up a program that feels as complicated as the rest of the fund put together even though it represents only 2% of the fund's assets.

We've structured our program to achieve broad diversification within the asset class. After much consideration, we decided to hire three managers of managers. These firms research and select a stable of commodity trading advisors (CTAs) and allocate funds among them. Each manager of managers may have six to 12 CTAs who have individual market specialties, styles and systems. A fund could go out and select its own CTAs, of course, but we felt that the size of our allocation to the asset class didn't warrant a separate, committed staff.

Our trading managers currently oversee 25 CTAs. Some have a technical investing approach; others are more fundamental. Some CTAs are very disciplined; others have a discretionary approach. Each of the three firms we hired has a different style of managing CTAs in different specialties. We've given them a high degree of autonomy in hiring, firing and reallocating assets among CTAs.

I concluded early on that we also needed help with custody and accounting. This is an asset class where you can execute thousands of trades a day; traditional custodial banks just aren't equipped to deal with this level of activity. We retain a consultant to provide back room accounting for the program. Through them, I know exactly how our program is faring during any given day. By mid-morning, I know where we ended the night before, net of all fees and expenses.

MANAGING THE DOWNSIDE: RISK CONTROLS

Each of our three trading managers establishes an automatic shut-down level for every CTA he supervises. We've set a similar maximum draw-down for each of the three managers and for the entire program. It's like a stop-loss: if they reach that point, they liquidate all positions. We have instant liquidity; these are very liquid markets.

At any point in time, we know exactly what our downside is, based on the signals from these circuit breakers. In fact, we have more risk control, and much more real time control, in this program than in any other asset class. Our consultant tracks how each CTA is doing. I get a daily report showing every CTA's performance for the prior day and for the month-to-date, quarter-to-date, year-to-date and program inception-to-date, as well as our position relative to stop-loss limits. Returns are all reported net of fees and transaction costs.

Since the program began, we've averaged about 600 trades a day. For the second quarter of 1994 it looks as if most of our traditional exposures will be down while the managed futures program will be up materially. One of the great attractions of this asset class is that the CTAs make money when they see trends, regardless of the direction of the trends. The traditional manager is at the mercy of the trend.

Because of the structure of our managed futures program, we spend very little time monitoring it in-house. The most time-consuming work was spent setting it up. There are reams of disclosure documents and contracts to review to get the accounts started, for example. But once the program is up and running, especially with the consultant on board providing the back room operation, it's very low maintenance.

COSTS: NEGOTIATING AGAINST A RETAIL MINDSET

The fees you'll hear quoted in this asset class are astronomical to anyone with an institutional viewpoint. Nowhere is Mellon Capital Management chairman Bill Fouse's observation about active management being akin to "monkeys trading bananas in a tree" more appropriate. These managers end up with a lot of bananas.

Futures developed as a retail product for high net worth individuals and the industry's retail mindset persists. We negotiated long and hard and achieved some significant movement, but the industry still has a long way to go in developing an institutional fee structure.

You can expect management fees on assets similar to what you'd pay on small-cap stocks and non-U.S. stocks, plus hefty performance fees based on trading profits. When we started looking, a typical quoted fee structure was 150 basis points on assets, plus a 20% incentive fee — a share in the profits. That's at the manager level. The CTA also has a flat fee based on the asset base plus a share of any profits.

Those were the fees we saw initially but, as I said, we negotiated hard and it's not where we ended up. Although we are paying an incentive fee, we established a performance hurdle that our managers must exceed before we start sharing the profits.

I would advise any fund investing in this asset class to focus on the negotiation with managers rather than with CTAs who have limited capacity. The very best traders are at capacity, and they simply won't negotiate. We leave the CTA fee negotiation to our managers.

One question often asked these days is, "How much capacity is there in the futures markets?" If every pension fund invested 1% in these markets, I don't think the futures exchanges would have the capacity to handle much more. And of course, the capacity of good traders is filled first. Even when we got into these markets, we couldn't get money to some of the best traders — they were closed. If you come into the futures markets late in the day, there's a real danger of being shut out or winding up having to bottom fish.

Most plan sponsors are only now starting to look at this asset class: the steep learning curve looms ahead. But conversations with colleagues around the country have convinced me that there's a lot of interest in managed futures and that pension fund investment in them will grow significantly during the rest of the decade.

Because we began studying this asset class three years ago, we were ready to make a commitment at a time when only a handful of pension funds and endowments were players. I believe it's always the plan sponsor's challenge and responsibility to be on the lookout for new things. There's an absolute premium for being receptive to new investment opportunities and seizing them early. We saw it with emerging markets, for example; those who went in early probably made the big killing. The fund managers I admire most — John Carroll at GTE, Gordon Binns, formerly at General Motor's fund, now on the board at the Virginia Retirement System, Doug Taylor and now Dick McGahan at Pacific Telesis Group — are always on the lookout for new opportunities and can be counted on to push the envelope of innovation. I believe the "newness" premium accrues to managers who approach investing in this necessary spirit of openness, innovation and prudence.

 SMART PILLS

> Involve the board or investment committee early: the learning curve is long and steep.

> Don't rely on traditional consultants to help you develop your strategy. Instead, talk to peers who've walked this road before as well as other industry experts.

> Don't expect your custodial bank to handle this asset class. Hire a consultant who knows it well.

> Negotiate management fees. But don't push too hard for lower fees at the trading level because the best traders command high fees.

ML Futures Investment Partners Inc.

A subsidiary of Merrill Lynch & Co., Inc.

Managed Futures Investment Services

Institutional and Corporate Clients

Jeffrey F. Chandor
Vice President
World Financial Center—South Tower
New York, NY 10080-6106
(212) 236-4170

RESOURCE GUIDE

THE INVESTORS PRESS RESOURCE GUIDE IS A SERIES OF SPECIAL SECTIONS INTENDED TO ENHANCE THE EDUCATIONAL VALUE OF THIS BOOK AND EXTEND ITS USEFULNESS AS A REFERENCE TOOL AND RESOURCE.

➤ UNDERWRITERS' PROFILES

➤ ANNOTATED BIBLIOGRAPHY

➤ GLOSSARY

➤ AUTHORS' BIOGRAPHIES

UNDERWRITER PROFILES

Angelo, Gordon & Co.
245 Park Avenue, New York, NY 10167
Phone: 212-692-2042 • Fax: 212-867-9328

Key Contact Information:
John M. Angelo, *Chief Executive Officer*
Michael L. Gordon, *Chief Operating Officer*
Marsha P. Roth, *Managing Director*

Year Founded: 1988

Total assets under management: $600 Million

Minimum account size: $25 Million (individual)
$1 Million (commingled)

Assets managed by client category:

	ASSETS MANAGED (in millions)
Corporate Funds	$150
Foundations & Endowments	75
Individuals	375

Special areas of expertise:
Non-traditional investment strategies in bankruptcy, distressed real estate, risk arbitrage, convertible hedging, utility hedging or their combinations.

Investment Approach:
Angelo, Gordon offers private and public foundations and endowment plans an expertise in creating absolute returns that utilize combinations of risk arbitrage, bankruptcy and distressed real estate. Additionally, the Firm seeks to generate a multiple of the Treasury rate by utilizing convertible bond hedging and/or a long/short electric utility strategy. The common thread that links all these investments is little or no correlation to stock or bond markets to limit downside risk. The implementation of these strategies is a conservative evaluation approach generated through in-depth research and a diversification strategy applied within each portfolio.

Barings
High Street Tower, 125 High Street, Suite 2700
Boston, MA 02110
Phone: 617-951-0052 • Fax: 617-951-1376

Key Contact Information:
Peter S. Hartley
Managing Director (US) 617-951-0052
M. Fraser Blakely
Director, Marketing 617-951-0052

Year Founded:
International management: 1979
Domestic management: 1967

Total tax-exempt assets under management from all sources:
Worldwide $43.7 Billion
North American based clients 10.7 Billion

Special areas of expertise:
Barings is a multi-dimensional, global asset management company specializing in global, international, regional and single country equity and fixed income management for clients worldwide.

Frequency of reporting results: Quarterly

Assets managed by client category:
(As relates to North American based clients only as of 6/30/94)

	NO. OF CLIENTS	ASSETS ($ millions)
Endowments	15	$ 283.5
Foundations	7	425.4
Publics	17	3,071.0
Corporates	47	4,469.1
Consultants	7	268.2
Other	29	2,212.2
Total	**122**	**10,729.4**

Investment approach:
• Top-down, centralized asset allocation
• Bottom-up, fundamental security selection
Barings' ultimate equity strategy is to find growing economies and companies at the right local valuation. Senior Asset Allocation Specialists formulate policy based on original research conducted by Regional Specialist teams located worldwide. Primary considerations for the equity process at both the country and stock levels are earnings growth, valuations and liquidity. Barings' fixed income process focuses on high sustainable real returns while controlling credit and currency risk.

Chancellor Capital Management, Inc.

1166 Avenue of the Americas, New York, NY 10036
Phone: 212-278-9000 • Fax: 212-278-9544

Key Contact Information:
Nina Lesavoy, *Head of Client Service
and New Business Development*   212-278-9664

Year founded:
1896; *an employee owned firm since April 1992*

**Total assets under
management from all sources:** $27.8 Billion*

Minimum account size: $ 2 Million
*(minimums may vary based upon product or whether account is
separately managed or commingled)*

Special areas of expertise:
Chancellor offers equity and fixed income investments
across the market capitalization spectrum. Equity
investments include large and small cap growth, core
(growth and value), market neutral and private equity.
Fixed income investments include full discretion,
enhanced cash, high yield and senior secured bank
loans. Combination products include balanced and
TAA portfolios.

Frequency of reporting results: Monthly

Assets managed by client category*:

	No. Clients Managed	Assets (in millions)
Corporate Funds	231	$14,200
Public Funds	37	4,700
Taft-Hartley Funds	15	600
Endowments & Foundations	54	900
Insurance	27	7,400

*As of 3/31/94

Investment approaches:
Chancellor believes that the highest quality investment management services can be provided to clients
through rigorous, repeatable processes. Our investment process is differentiated by a disciplined interplay of fundamental and quantitative resources. We
continually refine our investment processes to provide
consistently outstanding investment performance and
client service, tailored to the particular needs and
objectives of our clients.

Chicago Board of Trade

141 W. Jackson, Chicago, IL 60604
Phone: 312-435-7217 • Fax: 312-341-3027

Key Contact Information:
Patrick J. Catania, SVP, *Marketing*
James A. Borowicz, VP, *Marketing*

Organization:
The Chicago Board of Trade continues its leadership
role as the world's largest futures and options
exchange, setting another world record of 178 million
contracts traded in 1993. This record demonstrates
the important role the exchange plays in institutional
risk management strategies. Further, it is a direct trib-
ute to the ongoing confidence placed in the exchange
markets by its customers worldwide.

Product Specialty:
While the Chicago Board of Trade's U.S. Treasury
bond futures contract is the world's most actively
traded financial vehicle, current economic trends
have created record growth in three other Chicago
Board of Trade products, the two , five, and ten-year
U.S. Treasury note contracts. Most recently, the
Chicago Board of Trade launched a complex of
innovative new Flexible U.S. Treasury bond and note
futures options contracts. The new flexible options
provide investors with enhancements offered by
customized interest rate derivatives combined with
the security of exchange-traded products.

The Chicago Board of Trade provides its institutional customers with quality educational literature
focusing on the benefits and variety of applications
of futures and options for portfolio management,
including managed futures as an investment vehicle.

The Dreyfus Trust Company

144 Glenn Curtiss Boulevard
Uniondale, NY 11556-0144

Key Contact Information:

John E. Igneri
Sr. VP Sales-Corporations   212-922-8420

William E. Martin,
VP Sales-Endowments,
Foundations & Unions   212-922-8436

Year Founded: 1984

Total Assets Under Management/Administration:
     About $5 Billion

Special areas of expertise:

The Dreyfus Trust Company offers investment management services and products in a variety of investment disciplines, including: Small Cap, International Equity, International Recovery, Sector Rotation, Global and U.S. Fixed Income and Cash/Cash Equivalents.

Frequency of reporting results: Quarterly

Investment Approaches:

Small Cap: Fundamental, bottom-up investment style. Focus on companies with market cap below $750 million with dominant market positions, low-cost production, capital self-sufficiency and likelihood of benefitting from social/economic changes.

International Equity: Regional research teams cover international markets. Identify long-term value investments through rigorous bottom-up fundamental analysis combined with top-down economic, country and market research.

International Recovery: International returns can be enhanced through investing in the shares of companies experiencing difficulties, where we believe the market is undervaluing prospects for recovery. In searching for such deep value opportunities, market capitalization varies with small to medium companies dominant in the portfolio.

Sector Rotation: Large Company Growth, Large Company Value, Small Company Growth and Small Company Value.

Fixed Income: Value manager. Returns are enhanced through sector rotation and issue selection.

Fidelity Investments®

82 Devonshire Street, Boston, MA 02109

Key Contact Information:

Richard Malconian, *President*   617-563-5999
Thomas T. Bieniek, *Sr. Vice President*   617-563-5596
Lorrayne Yen Chu, *Sr. Vice President*   617-563-5998

Year Founded: 1946

Assets Under Management:

	NO. OF CLIENTS*	ASSETS*
Total FMR:	7M *shareholders*	$250 Billion
Total Tax-Exempt Services Company:	341,000 *shareholders* 12,000 institutions	$9.4 Billion

*as of 6/30/94

Special Areas of Expertise:

Large Cap Growth, Large Cap Value, Mid Cap Growth, Mid Cap Value, Balanced, Convertibles, Small Cap, Risk Controlled Equity, Fixed Income, Global Bond, High Yield, Alternative, International Equity, Risk Controlled International, Retirement Plan Services.

Investment Approach:

For all our disciplines, our investment philosophy is consistent with Fidelity's 48-year history.

Fundamental Research:

We base our decision-making on in-depth knowledge of companies and credits.

Adherence to Investment Disciplines:

A consistent, well thought out investment discipline governs each portfolio's objectives, investment universe, buy and sell disciplines, desired characteristics and expected performance pattern.

Fully Invested Portfolios:

Fidelity does not engage in market timing.

Portfolio Managers Have Responsibility and Accountability: Within their disciplines, portfolio managers have broad investment latitude and unlimited access to resources, and they are strictly accountable for performance.

Instinet Corporation

875 Third Avenue, New York, NY 10022
212-310-9500 • Fax: 212-838-8125

Key Contacts:
Davis Gaynes, *SVP Sales & Marketing*
Marc Gresack, *SVP International Sales & Trading*

Instinet Corporation provides global agency brokerage services to clients trading in over 30 countries on 5 continents. Instinet's strict neutrality ensures every client full anonymity, allowing institutions, broker-dealers and specialists to trade directly with each other on an equal footing. As a result, clients reduce the potential for market impact and frequently negotiate trades between the spread, reducing transaction costs. Instinet is registered with the U. S. Securities and Exchange Commission as a broker-dealer and is a member of the NASD. Affiliates of Instinet are members of: AMEX, U. S. Regional Exchanges, Chicago Board Options Exchange, Toronto Stock Exchange, London Stock Exchange, European Options Exchange (Amsterdam), Frankfurt Stock Exchange, Zurich Stock Exchange, the Paris Bourse and the Stock Exchange of Hong Kong.

Services:
- Equity trading in over thirty countries
- Trading in U. S. convertible bonds
- List trading for quantitative investors
- Real-time research and analytics
- Passive crossing services
- Soft and directed commission services
- Securities lending management

Offices:
New York, Toronto, London, Paris, Zurich, Frankfurt, Tokyo and Hong Kong

Merrill Lynch & Co.

Private Equity Group:
Kevin K. Albert, *Managing Director*   212-449-2012
William H. Riddle, Jr., *Director,*
Institutional Financial Services   212-449-7579

Equity Transactions: $7 Billion over two years

Investment Focus:
Institutional private equity placements with a focus on pooled limited partnership investment funds and direct issues of common or preferred stock. Investments typically offer higher returns than those otherwise available through public market investing. Investment opportunities include domestic and international offerings.

We have expertise in structuring transactions for the following investment categories:
- Management/Leveraged Buyouts
- International Growth Capital
- Turnaround/Distressed Situations
- Private Equity Growth Capital
- Real Estate

ML Futures Investment Partners Inc.
Jeffrey F. Chandor,
Director, Sales & Marketing   212-236-4170

Year founded: 1986

Assets under management: $1.4 Billion

Special areas of expertise:
ML Futures Investment Partners Inc. is one of the largest futures fund and program sponsors, offering these investments to individuals, pension and profit sharing plans and corporations. ML Futures Investment Partners Inc. retains the services of various Commodity Trading Advisors on behalf of the funds and programs to trade futures, forward contracts, currencies, securities and/or other derivatives in major markets of the global economy.

MetLife

One Madison Ave., New York, NY 10010

Key Contacts:

Harvey Young, *Sr. Vice President*   (212) 578-6287
Gene Murphy, *National Director*   (212) 578-8536

**Total tax-exempt assets under
management from all sources:** $77.5 Billion

**Wholly-Owned Investment Management
Subsidiaries:** State Street Research & Management
Company actively manages equity and fixed income
assets for individual and institutional separate accounts
and mutual funds. MetLife Investment Management
Corporation (MIMCO) provides active fixed income
management of diversified, mortgage-backed, asset-
backed, private placement, and duration constrained
portfolios for individual and commingled separate
accounts. GFM International Investors, Ltd., London
specializes in active non-U.S equity and fixed income
management of separate account and mutual fund
products.

Number of Clients (all sources):

Corporate Funds	1,303
Public Funds	113
Unions (Taft-Hartley)	89
Foundations & Endowments	8

Investment Approaches:
State Street Research draws upon specialized
internal research and "bottom-up" equity analysis. A
"top-down" fixed income philosophy utilizes interest
rate forecasting, yield curve analysis, and duration con-
straints. MIMCO achieves incremental return
to fixed income portfolios through duration management, sector weighting, issue selection, yield curve
analysis, and interest rate anticipation with emphasis
on credit and quantitative research. GFM's active
management strategy includes country allocation, currency weighting, and issue selection. In the firm's core
macroeconomic view, equity selections are based upon
fundamental valuation methods, while fixed income
issues are selected through the
variation of interest rate exposure, yield curve
analysis, and maturity structure.

NCM Capital Management Group, Inc.

103 West Main Street, Durham, NC 27701-3638
Phone: (919) 688-0620 • Fax: (919) 683-1352

Key Contact Information:
Maceo K. Sloan, CFA, *Chairman, President & CEO*
Justin F. Beckett, *Executive Vice President*
Clifford D. Mpare, CFA, *Senior Vice President*
Mary M. Ford, *Vice President*
Marc V. Reid, *Asst. Vice President*

Year founded: 1986

**Total tax-exempt assets under
management from all sources:**   over $2.5 Billion

Minimum account size: $10 Million (separate)
                             $1 Million (commingled)

Special areas of expertise:
Equity, fixed income, and balanced portfolio management emphasizing low-risk fundamentals.

Frequency of reporting results:
Monthly, Quarterly, Annually (per client request)

Assets managed by client category:

	No. OF CLIENTS	ASSETS MANAGED (*in millions*)
Corporate funds	16	$ 708
Public funds	33	1,537
Unions (Taft-Hartley)	14	218
Foundations & Endowments	9	73.5

Investment Approach:
NCM Capital's equity philosophy is *value* oriented,
employing a quantitative methodology to identify
stocks with low relative and absolute price earnings
ratios. We analyze positive earnings surprise and attractive earnings momentum relative to all other stocks in
our universe. NCM Capital's fixed income philosophy
is *quality* oriented, recognizing that most investors will
assume duration risk, but prefer insulation from the
extreme price volatility of low-quality fixed income
securities. Portfolios are invested in high-grade securities and managed within client-defined investment
objectives and risk parameters.

ANNOTATED BIBLIOGRAPHY

RECOMMENDATIONS FROM INVESTORS PRESS AND OUR AUTHORS

I. VENTURE CAPITAL

The New Venturers: Inside The High-Stakes World Of Venture Capital by John Wilson, (Reading, MA: Addison-Wesley Publishing Co., 1985). An absorbing history of venture capitalists that discusses the good, the bad and the ugly, and provides a vivid portrait of the culture.

Venture Capital: Law, Business Strategies And Investment Planning, by Joseph W. Bartlett, ed. (New York: John Wiley & Sons, 1988). This comprehensive volume provides valuable insights for the institutional investor on how venture capitalists operate. The author covers such issues as terms and conditions of private placements; torts, patents and licenses; how legal issues ultimately affect deals; and how and why you should take a company public.

"Silicon Valley: Window to the Future," by Gene Bylinsky, **High Tech**, Mary-Dawn Early, ed. (Hong Kong: Intercontinental Publishing Corporation, 1985). This glossy, lavishly photographed coffee-table book likens the rise of Silicon Valley to the California Gold Rush. Sections cover medicine, biology and genetic engineering as well as the development of the chip, software and lasers.

Venture Capital Manual: Investment/Strategy/Management by Steven James Lee, (Boston: Warren, Gorham & Lamont, Inc., 1991). This primer on venture capital comes in looseleaf form; an annual subscription entitles readers to updates from a large roster of contributing editors.

Other worthwhile publications include:

Private Equity Analyst, a 12-page monthly newsletter published by Asset Alternatives, Wellesley, MA, 617-431-7353, covers the private equity market, venture capital, LBOs and mezzanine funds. Each issue features fundraising and industry news with contact names plus two or three analytical articles. A popular, lower-priced alternative to **Venture Capital Journal**, though narrower in scope.

Two noteworthy articles by Tom Judge of AT&T: "Season Opener: Annual Meetings Need to Be Made More Productive," the cover story in **Private Equity Analyst's** March 1992 issue, suggests what ought to be on the agenda of every annual meeting along with how to allocate meeting time effectively and how to prepare for these meetings. In the September 1993 issue's "Financial Reports from GPs Need to Be Improved," Mr. Judge discusses ways venture firms can make financial reports more timely, more consistent and easier to use.

Venture Capital Timesaver, is a monthly digest of venture capital publications. Created by consultant Dick Radez of Russell & Co., Westport, CT as an information source for clients, **Venture Capital Timesaver** provides a good overview of the domestic venture capital market. **Red Herring**, a monthly magazine introduced in 1993, is a solid source that concentrates on IPOs and later-stage ventures in the high-tech sector. 415-780-9070. **Asian Venture Capital Journal**, a quarterly, is published by Ullmer Bros., New York. **Venture One** offers a database of venture-financed companies which tracks key investment statistics from the limited and general partners' perspectives. Contact David Gleba, 415-621-1200.

Venture Economics, New York, 212-765-5311, a leading information source on venture capital, publishes numerous directories and periodicals:

Pratt's Guide To Venture Capital Sources is an annual directory of venture capital firms organized alphabetically by state. It also includes some foreign venture capital firms. Lists personnel contacts, as well as preferred types of financings and investment criteria. **Pratt's Buyouts Guide To Financing Sources**, another annual directory, lists equity and mezzanine providers and senior lenders. **Investment Benchmarks Report: Venture Capital**, also annual, is the only comprehensive source of performance data known to our author-experts, with details on performance of various partnerships by grouping, year, industry and stage. **Venture Capital Journal**, a monthly publication of Venture Economics, is the granddaddy of venture capital magazines, covering primarily the U.S. venture capital market and other private equity markets. It focuses on news and fundraising developments. **Buyouts**, a semi-monthly newsletter, is the only trade publication that focuses exclusively on news and fundraising developments in the LBO market. **European Venture Capital Journal**, and the **U.K. Venture Capital Journal**, are the European and U.K. counterparts of **Venture Capital Journal**. Each appears six times a year.

II. DERIVATIVES

Institutional Investor offers three useful publications:

Derivatives Week, a weekly newsletter, provides international coverage of the derivatives industry. Call 1-800-543-4444 or 212-303-3233. The editors have compiled useful columns to date in book form with **Learning Curves: The Guide To Understanding Derivatives**, (New York: Institutional Investor, Inc., 1994). **The Journal of Derivatives**, is II's respected quarterly review.

Derivatives Strategy, a semi-monthly newsletter, is designed to help pension funds and money managers use derivatives to their best advantage. Edited/published by Joe Kolman, 212-366-9578.

Probus Publishing Company, a Chicago-based financial publisher, offers a number of educational titles on derivatives, including:

Dictionary Of Financial Risk Management, by Gary L. Gastineau, (1992). Gastineau, a premier options expert formerly with Swiss Bank Corporation, adeptly explains arcane concepts in understandable terms. **Managed Futures: Performance, Evaluation And Analysis Of Commodity Funds, Pools And Accounts**, edited by Carl C. Peters (1992). Among the many valuable articles within this volume is a groundbreaking study by John Lintner, "The Potential Role of Managed Commodity-Financial Futures Accounts (and/or Funds) in Portfolios of Stocks and Bonds," originally presented at the Financial Analysts Federation's 1983 annual conference. Other resources to explore: **Handbook Of Derivative Instruments: Investment, Research, Analysis & Portfolio Applications**, edited by Atsuo Konishi and Ravi Dattatreya, (1991); **Handbook Of Derivatives & Synthetics: Innovations, Technologies & Strategies In The Global Markets** by Robert A. Klein and Jess Lederman, (1994); **Eurodollar Futures & Options**, by Galen Burghardt and M. Lane, (1991); and **Option Volatility And Pricing Strategies:**

YOUR EMPLOYEES MAY
HAVE A FEW QUESTIONS
ABOUT THEIR DC PLAN

WE HAVE MORE THAN 100 ANSWERS

*I*t's not surprising that plan participants have lots of questions about their Defined Contribution Plan–how it works; what they can expect to withdraw from it, and when; how to make the most sensible investments for their specific needs; whether or not they should even enroll.

As evidence mounts that employees of U.S. companies are not investing early enough, wisely enough or simply **enough**, corporate sponsors have an increasingly urgent obligation to respond by giving their employees a solid basis for making sound decisions about their futures.

That's why this new book from Investors Press is so important.

Building Your Nest Egg

Scrupulously researched by the editors of Investors Press, *Building Your Nest Egg* is based on interviews with more than 100 large and mid-range companies. In concise, layman's language, the book provides an objective, third party response to 100 of the most important and frequently asked employee questions about 401(k) plans. The answers will help *your* employees make more informed judgments about the value of enrolling early, the amount they should commit and which investment vehicles will best meet their specific needs and expectations.

In addition to the Q&A, the book features a discussion by Contributing Editor Theodore Benna, widely known as "the father of 401(k)," who shares his unique knowledge of employee questions and concerns. Throughout the book's 144 pages of text, tables, charts and graphs clarify the more complex aspects of investing. Easy to understand, thorough and relevant to participants' practical needs, *Building Your Nest Egg* is an ideal way for corporate plan sponsors to supply the independent guidance their employees need to plan responsibly for their retirement.

To reserve your complimentary copy of Building Your Nest Egg, ***please fax your request to Investors Press (203) 868-9733.***
(Publication date: Spring, 1995)

Advanced Trading Techniques For Professionals, by Sheldon Natenberg, (Revised edition 1994).

A few other noteworthy suggestions:

Managed Futures: An Investor's Guide, by Beverly Chandler (New York: John Wiley & Sons, 1994).

The Institutional Investors' Guide To Managed Futures Programs by Stephen M. Douglass (New York: McGraw-Hill, 1994).

Fundamentals Of Investments by Gordon J. Alexander, William F. Sharpe, and Jeffery V. Bailey (Englewood Cliffs, NJ: Prentice Hall, Second edition, 1993). Chapters 24-26 are especially instructive.

The growing use of derivatives and the question of whether they pose a risk to the global financial system have been the subject of much attention in the general media as well as within the industry. A few useful articles presenting the pros and cons:

"Managed Futures White Paper," by John McLaren, Nancy E. Everett and Thomas J. O'Donnell. This paper was presented at the Chicago Mercantile's Fourth Annual Managed Futures Symposium in 1992. The authors, investment officers with the Virginia Retirement System, originally presented the paper to their board of trustees as their case for adopting a managed futures investment program.

"What Institutions Want in Managed Futures Programs," by Richard Pike, **Futures**, November 1991. Pike, a leading authority on managed futures, is consultant to several major pension funds including the San Diego County Employees' Retirement Association.

"The Essentials of Financial Risk Management," by Gary L. Gastineau, **Financial Analysts Journal**, (September/October 1993), 17-21. Gastineau demystifies market risk associated with derivatives and thus addresses recent concerns of regulators.

"The Risk That Won't Go Away," by Carol Loomis, **Fortune**, March 7, 1994. This cover story offers a rational, if negative, look at derivatives investing and its impact on the global economy.

"The Age of Digital Capitalism," by Robert Lenzner, **Forbes**, March 29, 1993. Another cover story that takes a sober view of derivatives.

"Why Plan Sponsors Should Include Managed Futures in Pension Portfolios," by Robert J. Samples, **Pension World**, November 1993, 34-35.

"More Put their Faith in Futures," by Barry B. Burr, **Pensions & Investments**, March 21, 1994. A roundup of new entrants to the managed futures investment arena.

"Derivatives: Why Bother?" by Lars Toomre and Christopher Li, MetLife Investment Management Corporation (MIMCO). Critics state that derivatives are nothing more than a financial pyramid of interlocking, highly leveraged transactions that put the entire financial system at risk. Advocates argue that the benefits of derivatives far outweigh their potential hazards and that these instruments are highly effective in helping financial institutions and plan sponsors manage their respective risks. This paper addresses the characteristics of derivative instruments and explains how derivatives can alter the risk/reward profile of fixed-income portfolios. Fax article request (**#IP005**) to Jennifer Karpiel at MetLife, 212-578-7175.

III. ECONOMICALLY TARGETED INVESTMENTS

Interpretive Bulletin No. 94-1, issued by the Department of Labor, Pension and Welfare Benefits Administration, June 23, 1994 reaffirms the Department's long-held position that Economically Targeted Investments are consistent with Federal pension law as long as they offer an expected rate of return commensurate with comparable investments with similar risks. The Department is establishing a national clearinghouse of ETI activity. The Bulletin is available from the DOL's Office of Public Disclosure: 202-219-8771.

"Tapping Pension Power to Rebuild America Inc.," by Stephen E. Clark, *Institutional Investor*, March 1992, 45-49.

"Defining the ETI Debate," by Ronald D. Watson, *Plan Sponsor*, May 1994, 70-71. Watson of Custodial Trust Company chairs the DOL ERISA Advisory Committee which studied ETIs for two years.

"Economically Targeted Investments: A New Threat to Private Pension Funds," by M. Wayne Marr, John R. Nofsinger and John L. Trimble, *Journal of Applied Corporate Finance*, (Summer 1993), 91-95.

"Economically Targeted Investments," by M. Wayne Marr, John R. Nofsinger and John L. Trimble, *Financial Analysts Journal*, (March/April 1994), 7-8. More anti-ETI arguments.

"Economically Targeted Investment: Real Estate Strategies for Pension Funds," by James R. DeLisle and Kurt Wright, Equitable Life Assurance Society White Paper Series: Volume 5, August 1992.

The Center for Policy Alternatives, Washington, DC, 202-387-6030, has studied ETIs extensively. Among its reports:
"Economically Targeted Investments by Statewide Public Pension Fund Systems," by Richard Ferlauto and Jeffrey Clabourn, 1993. "The Fiduciary Duty Aspects of Economically Targeted Investments," by Richard Ferlauto, 1993. "Economically Targeted Investments: Rebuilding America's Communities" Conference Report, 1994.

IV. DISTRESSED INVESTMENTS

Bankruptcy And Distressed Restructurings: Analytical Issues And Investment Opportunities, edited by Edward I. Altman, New York University Salomon Center Series, (Homewood, IL: BusinessOne Irwin, 1992). Prominent practitioners and academics explore such topics as bankruptcy and liquidation costs and their impact on corporate values, the evaluation of investor priorities and market efficiencies, and what determines successful distressed exchange issues. The author is a leading international authority on corporate bankruptcy.

Distressed Securities: Analyzing And Evaluating Market Potential And Investment Risk, by Edward I. Altman, (Chicago, IL: Probus Publishing Company, 1991). The author draws on the practical experience of a small group of investors over several decades.

Investing In Financially Distressed Firms: A Guide To Pre- And Post-Bankruptcy Opportunities, by Murali Ramaswami and Susan E. Moeller, (Westport, CT: Quorum Books, 1990).

V. ALTERNATIVE INVESTMENTS – GENERAL

"Reaching for Return," by Andrew Sollinger, *Institutional Investor,* April 1994. This case study of how Delmarva Power & Light's pension fund considered adding market neutral hedge funds and timberland to its allocation exemplifies the trend among plan sponsors to bolster returns via alternative asset classes once considered too risky.

"Market Neutral: A Strategy for All Seasons?" by Edward R. Finch, Senior Vice President, Portfolio Manager, State Street Research & Management Company. Designed to outperform cash and intermediate bonds, market-neutral investing has begun to gain attention as a versatile alternative/enhancement to traditional asset classes. Market-neutral managers carefully match long and short equity positions to construct a portfolio with low volatility. Can this strategy really add value on a consistent basis? The author believes it can, even in today's challenging environment. Fax article request **(# IP006)** to J.J. Milder at State Street, 617-951-9919.

"The High Yield Market Today," by Heather O'Loughlin, Portfolio Analyst, Fidelity Investments. Although high yield bonds are not typically classified as an alternative investment, increasing numbers of investors are attracted to the similar benefits in this investment class. This paper defines high yield bonds, provides background on the high yield market, and gives reasons why investors should consider this type of investment. Fax article request **(# IP007)** to Sandy McCarthy at Fidelity Investments, 617-476-3837.

"Assessing Alternative Investments," by Raphael Berber, Kathleen Young and Robert Ryan, *Pension Executive Review*, January 1991. The authors present an overview for plan sponsors who are considering alternative investment allocation strategies.

"Private Market Investing," by Raphael Berber, *Pension Executive Review*, October 1991, reviews issues faced by pension plans as a result of asset size, the risk/return characteristics of the private market, and the evolution of pension fund participation in this market.

"Where are We? The Truth and Nothing But the Truth," by Stephen M. McLean (1994) provides a current analysis of U.S. markets and the supply and demand for partnership capital. Fax requests for above three articles to **(# IP008)** to William H. Riddle, Jr. at Merrill Lynch & Co., 212-449-7969.

"Managed Futures and the Asset Allocation Process," by Randi E. Simon, *Pension Executive Review*, January 1991, analyzes the risk/return characteristics of managed futures in a traditionally structured portfolio. Fax article request **(# IP009)** to Jeffrey Chandor at Merrill Lynch at 212-236-4796.

Many of the conference proceedings and monographs published by the Association For Investment Management and Research, (AIMR) Charlottesville, VA, provide information on a wide variety of investment topics from leading experts. A few offerings on alternative investments: "Investing in Venture Capital" (1989), "Analyzing Investment Opportunities in Distressed and Bankrupt Companies" (1991), "Options & Futures: A Tutorial" (1992), "Derivative Strategies for Managing Portfolio Risk" (1993), and "Managed Futures and the Investment Portfolio" (1994). Call 1-800-789-AIMR.

For complimentary copies of the following Chicago Board of Trade publications, call 1-800-THE-CBOT, ext. 80:

Managed Futures: An Alternative Investment Opportunity. This brief pamphlet explains the benefits of participation, the types of investment opportunities available, and the financial integrity of the underlying futures markets.

Treasury Futures for Institutional Investors. This 107-page book provides an in-depth view of the Treasury futures market. Topics include equating cash and Treasury futures price movements, applying risk-management strategies, enhancing returns on a portfolio, and spread trading, plus an overview of U.S. regulations governing the use of futures contracts.

Futures: The Realistic Hedge for the Reality of Risk. A 16-page booklet that examines aspects of the futures industry from grains to worldwide financial markets. Concepts covered include the auction system, the function of volatility and liquidity in the market, price-risk management strategies, and preserving market integrity.

ORGANIZATIONS & ASSOCIATIONS

National Venture Capital Association, a trade and lobbying group for venture capitalists, is becoming more attentive to the limited partner community, 703-351-5269.

Institutional Limited Partners Association is an informal group of over 40 institutional investors that meets twice a year to discuss important issues in venture investing. Co-founded in 1990 by Tom Judge of AT&T, membership is limited to active investors; gatekeepers are excluded. Contact Solomon Owayda (1994 chairman) at California State Teachers' Retirement System, 916-387-3752.

CONFERENCE ORGANIZATIONS

Venture capital gatherings include the *Venture Economics* Venture Forum and Buyout Symposium, 212-765-5311, ext. 215; meetings sponsored by the International Business Forum (IBF), 212-279-2525; and the National Association of Small Business Investment Companies, 703-683-1601.

Conferences on alternative investments are held by such organizations as Institutional Investor (Institute meetings, 212-303-3641), (Asset Allocation Symposia, 212-303-3510); and the Institute for Fiduciary Education (IFE), 916-922-1100.

The Chicago Board of Trade, the Chicago Board Options Exchange, and the London International Financial Futures Exchange co-sponsor an annual Risk Management Conference covering futures and options. Contact Jo Ellen Schroedter, 312-341-3104.

Conferences on managed futures include: The Chicago Mercantile Exchange's Annual Managed Futures Symposium, 312-930-3449; the Managed Futures Association's Annual Conference, 415-325-4533; and meetings or workshops sponsored by *Managed Account Reports*, the leading trade publication on managed futures, 212-213-6202.

G L O S S A R Y

Alpha: A coefficient that measures the investment return of a particular stock relative to the S&P 500. Alpha represents the inherent value of the investment as opposed to returns caused by external factors such as volatility. An alpha of 0 is equal to the S&P average dividend return. A positive alpha of 5, for example, means that the stock will yield a return 5% greater than the S&P average. Many plan sponsors believe that the investment manager's primary responsibility is to deliver as much alpha as possible — the incremental return above agreed-upon benchmarks.

Alternative Investments: Asset classes other than the traditional categories of stocks, bonds and cash such as venture capital, oil and gas and derivatives.

Arbitrage: The practice of buying and selling the same security, currency or commodity in different marketplaces to capitalize on price disparities. Another type of arbitrage involves buying one security linked to a short sale of the same security.

Beta: A coefficient that measures a stock's volatility relative to the stock market as a whole. The S&P 500 Index has a beta of 1; a stock with a higher beta is more volatile than the market and one with a lower beta is less volatile than the market.

Buyout: The purchase of a company's stock, or a controlling portion of it, to take over its assets and operations. Buyouts can be made through a tender offer or through negotiation. A Leveraged Buyout (LBO) is a type of corporate takeover that utilizes borrowed funds. Typically, the LBO uses the target company's assets as collateral for the loan financing the buyout. The acquirer repays the loan from cash flow generated by the acquired company.

Carried Interest, or Carry: In venture capital vernacular, the 20% of profits allocated to the general partner as a performance management incentive.

Correlation: How the returns of one asset class or investment correlate with those of another. Common stocks and venture capital, for example, both represent corporate equity and correlate more closely than do common stocks and Treasury bills. One objective of asset diversification is to reduce correlation, so that when the value of one asset is declining, the value of the other is rising. A measure of this relationship is called the "correlation coefficient."

Dollar Cost Averaging (Dollar Averaging): A way to build assets by investing a set amount of money in securities at fixed intervals, buying more when the share price is low and less when it is high. The overall cost is therefore lower than it would be if a constant number of shares were bought at regular intervals.

Due Diligence: Strictly speaking, a meeting of prospective members of an underwriting syndicate and the officers of the issuing corporation at which underwriters can ask questions about the issuer's background, financial reliability and plans for the proceeds. Required by the SEC, the due diligence meeting must take place between preliminary registration and the effective offering date. In a general sense, due diligence refers to the entire process of researching and verifying the soundness of a potential issuer or investment.

Duration: Variously defined, its more modern meaning is the point when the (paper) loss of bond principal equals the increased return from the reinvestment of coupon income if interest rates were to rise. Duration is an important concept in bond portfolio management associated with tempering interest rate risk.

Early Stage Investment: A venture investment which is later than seed stage and usually funds a going concern. Most often the company is not profitable and it may or may not have revenues.

Economically Targeted Investing (ETIs): A type of investing, largely made by public pension funds, whose goal is to spur economic growth in addition to achieving returns. Not to be confused with "social investing" (e.g., Green funds) which seeks to achieve a socially benevolent goal.

Gatekeeper: A money management firm that invests and monitors capital for institutional clients, targeting the private equity industry in both limited partnerships and direct investments. A gatekeeper usually has a large pool of capital and can exert significant impact on a partnership's ability to raise capital and on its terms and conditions. For small institutions lacking the in-house capability to invest in venture capital, gatekeepers provide valuable access to the venture market. However, the level of fees paid to general partners remains a controversial issue.

General Partner (GP): That partner of a limited partnership who is responsible for the day-to-day operations of the partnership and any debts it assumes. Although the GP has unlimited liability, he receives fees and often retains a percentage of ownership in the partnership.

Hedge Fund: In limited partnerships hedge funds speculate in securities, often using arbitrage strategies. Limited partners have limited risk; the rewards are shared by the general partners. A hedge fund can also be a mutual fund that uses derivative instruments such as options or futures, to hedge risk.

Incentive Fee: The fee awarded a general partner in a limited partnership for reaching or surpassing a returns goal.

Later Stage: See **Mezzanine Investing**.

Leverage: The degree of debt a company has in relation to its equity. Financial leverage is beneficial to shareholders as long as the return on the borrowed money exceeds the cost of interest and the market value of their shares rises. In popular terms a "leveraged company" is one that is "highly leveraged" or has an excessive degree of debt capitalization.

Limited Liability Company (LLC): A cross between a partnership and a corporation, it has the tax and liability advantages of each. The liability to loss beyond contributed capital is strictly limited. In addition, the investor can exercise control. LLCs are easily established offshore.

Limited Partner (LP): An investor in a vehicle organized to raise capital for a start-up or early stage company. LPs invest money but have limited liability, no involvement in day-to-day management, and cannot lose more than their dollar investment. They receive income, capital gains and tax benefits. The most common types of limited partnerships are real estate and oil and gas; others might include movies and R&D investments.

Mezzanine Investing: Investment in a going concern which typically has revenues and has not yet gone public. A mezzanine investment may or may not be profitable, but the risk of loss is reduced. Often, financing funds the ramp up in sales or bridges a company's growth to more mainstream financing options such as bank loans or public markets.

Placement Fee: The fee charged by a placement agent to raise a fund; typically in the range of 1 to 2% of total proceeds.

Private Equity: Any of a variety of equity investments which are not publicly traded or subject to SEC regulation including limited partnerships, LBOs, restructurings and direct investments.

Real Assets: In venture capital terms, tangible assets, such as real estate, minerals, timber, oil and gas, as opposed to equity or debt.

Seed Investment: Early stage investing in a start-up company, usually at the point when there is little more than proprietary technology or a business plan. The investment can be a loan or an investment in convertible bonds or preferred stock. The investor gains an equity stake in the company in return for his investment.

Vintage Year Performance: A method of performance measurement of partnerships, conceived by AT&T's Tom Judge in 1987 and adopted as a standard by Venture Economics' annual Investment Benchmarks report, it compares the performance of partnerships started in the same year, assuming they all invested during the same time frame. Because the total universe of partnerships is so relatively small, it is not useful to compare partnerships within the same industry or sector.

AUTHORS' BIOGRAPHIES

Erica C. Bushner became Director of Venture Capital and Alternative Investments for the Pennsylvania State Employes' Retirement System (SERS) in 1989. The fund currently has over $257 million in commitments to 22 domestic venture capital limited partnerships and $235 million committed to more than a dozen private equity partnerships. Since joining SERS in 1983, Ms. Bushner has served as System Analyst, Chief of Accounting Control, Chief Internal Auditor and Staff Assistant to the Executive Director. She holds a bachelor's degree in Accounting and has an MBA from Pennsylvania State University. A Certified Public Accountant (CPA) and Chartered Financial Analyst (CFA), Ms. Bushner is a member of several industry associations and venture investing groups, including the Central Pennsylvania Investment Managers Association of which she is currently president. She is also an arbitrator for the National Association of Securities Dealers.

Carmen J. Gigiliotti, Portfolio Manager-Venture Investments, is responsible for all investing in alternative asset classes for the E. I. DuPont de Nemours & Co. Pension Trust Fund including real estate, distressed debt, corporate finance and venture capital. Before joining DuPont in 1992, he was a Vice President with First Westinghouse Capital Corporation, a subsidiary of Westinghouse Credit Corporation, where he spent four years making direct investments in private placements of subordinated debt and equity. From 1984 to 1988, Mr. Gigliotti was Assistant Vice President - Mergers and Acquisitions at PNC Merchant Banking, a subsidiary of PNC Financial in Pittsburgh. At PNC, he advised the bank's clients on acquisition and divestiture transactions and assisted with acquisition financing and transaction valuation and structuring. Mr. Gigliotti, a Certified Public Accountant, was with Price Waterhouse from 1978 until 1984 where his last assignment was as tax manager. He earned his B.S. in Biology at Pennsylvania State University and his M.B.A. at the University of Pittsburgh.

Thomas B. Judge is Vice President and Director of Alternative Investments of the AT&T Investment Management Corporation, the entity that oversees the $40 billion AT&T pension fund. He is responsible for the fund's venture capital, natural resource and non-traditional investments. Over the past 14 years he has committed $1.3 billion to venture capital with 87 venture firms throughout the world. Mr. Judge has been with AT&T for 39 years and has, during those four decades, administered all facets of the funded corporate benefit plan assets. Widely acknowledged among institutional investors as the dean of venture capital, he has made such important contributions to the field as devising performance benchmarks and developing policy and fee structures. Mr. Judge serves on the advisory board of ten venture capital firms. He is co-founder and past Chairman of the Institutional Limited Partners Association (ILPA), the prestigious group of institutional investors active in venture capital. He is a frequent speaker at industry conferences and seminars including the Venture Economics Venture Forum and the National Venture Capital Association Annual Meetings, as well as at the Institute for International Research and the International Business Forum venture capital conferences, organizations for which he serves as an advisor. Mr. Judge recently authored published articles on venture capital annual meetings and venture firm reporting. (See Annotated Bibliography.)

Douglas K. Park, Director of Private Transactions/Venture Capital at Ameritech, has put his own stamp on Ameritech's venture investment program since he took its helm in 1991. Today he oversees a portfolio of some $650 million in 98 limited partnerships and direct investments. An active member of the private equity investment community, Mr. Park participates in ILPA and is a frequent panelist at industry conferences. He also serves on many investment partnership advisory boards. Previously, Mr. Park was a Senior Investment Manager at Citicorp Venture Capital, Ltd. where he directed acquisition financings and the investment program dedicated to venture capital partnerships. From 1986 to 1988 he managed the $200 million venture capital program at the Mutual of New York, focusing on terms and conditions of investment partnerships to improve results for the limited partners. Previously he held positions in corporate finance and portfolio management at W.R. Grace and Prudential Capital Markets. Mr. Park earned a B.A. in Biology and an M.B.A. in Finance from Columbia University.

Richard N. Rose joined the San Diego County Employees' Retirement Association in 1993 as the System's first Chief Investment Officer with staff responsibility for its $2.2 billion in assets. Previously, he served as a private consultant to another public pension fund and before that, he spent ten years with Pacific Telesis Group and its predecessor, the Pacific Telephone and Telegraph Company. During his tenure at PacTel, Mr. Rose held numerous positions in financial management, both during and after the divestiture of the Bell System, including that of Manager-Investment Administration for the firm's $10 billion pension fund. A strong advocate of derivatives in the institutional portfolio, Mr. Rose created a $430 million model portfolio of derivative investments for the proceeds of San Diego County's Pension Obligation Bond issue in February 1994. Under his direction, SDCERA has become one of the few public or private pension funds to initiate a managed futures program. He is also a vocal proponent of non-U.S. equities in the pension portfolio and believes that an allocation of less than 20 to 30% of plan assets to this class borders on imprudence. Mr. Rose earned his B.A. in Economics at the University of California at Berkeley and his M.B.A. in Finance (with Honors) at San Francisco State University.

Sallie Shuping Russell is Vice President and Investment Director of Duke Management Company where she oversees the investment of over 12% of Duke University's endowment pool and 10% of its retirement fund in venture capital, leveraged buyouts, restructurings and other private equity vehicles. As a member of the Company's Investment Strategy Committee, she helps to develop overall investment objectives for the funds, build asset allocation models, select public security and real estate managers and monitor overall portfolio performance. Before the formation of the Duke Management Company in 1990, Ms. Russell was an Assistant Vice President at Duke University where she worked with the Executive Vice President to oversee the investment, business and administrative functions of the University. Ms. Russell was previously a Vice President of McMillion/Eubanks, a money management firm in Greensboro, North Carolina and before that, a consultant at Cambridge Associates in Boston. Ms. Russell received her M.B.A. from Columbia University and her B.A. in English and Political Science from the University of North Carolina, Chapel Hill.

David VanBenschoten has been Vice President, Director of Finance – Investments at General Mills, Inc. since 1992. He oversees the investment and financial administration of General Mills' $1.8 billion retirement plan assets and has responsibility for approximately $500 million of long-term corporate marketable investments. Mr. VanBenschoten joined General Mills in 1979 after he earned his bachelor's degree in Economics at Bethel College in Minnesota and completed his graduate work in Business Administration at the University of Minnesota. He began as a Financial Analyst and advanced as Manager-Benefit Finance, Director-Marketable Securities, Director-Investment Management and Assistant Treasurer before assuming his current responsibilities. Mr. VanBenschoten was among the first pension investment officers to use financial futures and options in the pension portfolio in the early 1980s. A member of the Financial Executive Institute's Committee on Investment of Employee Benefit Assets (CIEBA), Mr. VanBenschoten is also a Trustee of the Baptist General Conference/Bethel College Retirement Plans Trust.

David A. White has been Treasurer and Chief Investment Officer of the $2.3 billion Rockefeller Foundation since 1991. Previously, as Staff Vice President-Capital Management at Unisys, he oversaw $5.7 billion in employee benefit assets for that corporation's worldwide pension and savings plans. After earning his B.A. and M.B.A. from the University of Michigan, Mr. White held a variety of positions in finance, accounting, control and planning at Unisys and its predecessors from 1971 to 1981. His passion for investments has consistently inspired him toward innovation; he implemented the first large-scale institutional long/short (market neutral) stock strategy and one of the first options-based currency overlay strategies, and made the Rockefeller Foundation among the first endowed private foundations to issue rated tax-exempt bonds. His investment philosophy includes a firm belief in investing with the mentality of a principal. Since 1988 Mr. White has implemented such skill-based strategies as currency hedge funds, leveraged mortgage arbitrage, risk arbitrage and leveraged fixed income futures arbitrage. A founding member of the Financial Executive Institute's Committee for the Investment of Employee Benefit Assets (CIEBA), Mr. White is also a member of the board of The Investment Fund for Foundations (TIFF).

OTHER 1994 INVESTORS PRESS
INVESTMENT MANAGEMENT BOOKS

THE CHANGING FACE
OF PENSION MANAGEMENT:
*Rescripting the Role of Plan Sponsors, Trustees,
Money Managers and Consultants*

May 1994

A WING AND A PRAYER:
*Defined Contribution Plans and the
Pursuit of 24 Karat Golden Years*

August 1994

EMERGING MARKETS:
A Map for Global Investors

December 1994

COPIES OF FILLING THE VACUUM ARE AVAILABLE FOR $45 EACH INCLUDING TAX, HANDLING AND SHIPPING COSTS. PLEASE ALLOW THREE WEEKS FOR DELIVERY. PLEASE SPECIFY QUANTITY AND OTHER TITLES YOU ARE ORDERING. PAYMENT AND MAILING INSTRUCTIONS SHOULD BE MAILED TO:

INVESTORS
PRESS

INVESTORS PRESS BOOKS
P.O. BOX 1286
WASHINGTON, CT 06793